What Others Say about Pitch Yourself

'The reality is that ALL candidates need to engage in 'selling' their product (transferable skills and competencies) to their target market (employers). *Pitch Yourself* shows how to accomplish this.'
Ken Keeley, PhD, Executive Director, Career Opportunities Center, Carnegie Mellon University, Tepper School of Business US

'*Pitch Yourself* shows people how to think differently about themselves and then demonstrate to an employer the transferable assets and experience that we all have, in a convincing and relevant manner.'
Keith Faulkner CBE, Managing Director, Working Links (Employment) Ltd, UK

'I hope it becomes industry standard'
Jack Gratton, CEO Major Players – leading marketing recruitment agency (London)

'I wish other candidates would use an Elevator Pitch'
Ivor Yeshin, Head of HR for T-Mobile (Europe)

'The thinking behind *Pitch Yourself* truly gets under the skin of what job search is all about. The emphasis on preparation is key to knowing your personal story and knowing how to present only the strongest and most relevant aspects of this story to potential employers. The advice and guidance is direct and to the point and will not only help those looking for a job but also help all those recruiting.'
Hugh Lailey, Director of Career Management Centre, Erasmus Rotterdam School of Management, Netherlands

'The Faust's approach is applicable in all facets of job hunting from self evaluation to the interview ... robust, well thought out and easy to communicate.'
Andrew Jackson, Head of Employer Relations, Cass Business School, City University, London

'A refreshing approach'
Simon Tankard, Head of Careers at Oxford SAID Business School UK

'The Personal Elevator Pitch is a refreshing change to the traditional – soon to be outdated – chronological CV. The book applies up-to-date marketing techniques to promote people into their new careers. A must for anyone.'
Katty Ooms Suter, Director MBA Career Services, IMD Switzerland

'When students first meet employers in a pre-interview setting they have to sell themselves, in 60 seconds or less, with sound bites that express the transferable assets of value to the employer.'
Karin Ash, MBA Director Cornell, Johnson Graduate School of Management, US

'Read this self-marketing book (and again), you'll be so much more convincing if put into action.'
Marc Smelik, Director, Career Management Centre, Leeds University Business School, UK

'I can see any candidate from graduates to seasoned business professionals benefiting.'
Chris Bristow, Director of Postgraduate Management Programmes, Kent Business School, UK

'The traditional CV sucks the personality out of the words and it becomes a shadow of a candidate's promise. The Elevator Pitch breathes life back and is grounded in hard evidence. Since I've been recommending the Faust's book I've seen some fabulous pitches.'
Angela Harris, Careers Management Centre, London Business School, UK

'The feedback has been outstandingly positive, and I'm now seeing some truly vibrant and targeted Elevator Pitches and personal profiles.'
Carri Nicholson, MBA Programme Manager, Durham Business School, UK

'The Faust brothers have given us the first piece of eminently sensible new thinking in years on how to re-write your CV. It's truly the way forward'
Daniel Ganly, MBA Director at Oxford Brookes University UK

'A lively and innovative approach'
Patricia Quinn,Head of Careers and Employment, Sheffield Hallam University, UK

'By applying valuable guidelines from the world of marketing to the job application process, Pitch Yourself can help graduates think in terms of an effective sales pitch of their transferable assets, rather than a bland list of what they have done.'
Brian Nisbet, Director Career Development & Employment Centre, University of Sussex, UK

'Ever felt frustrated by your CV's inability to sell the real you? Worry no more. The Elevator Pitch can really transform the way you're seen by prospective employers. Do yours now before everyone else cottons on.'
Tom Vick, Managing Director, dfgw - the leading London advertising agency

Pitch
Yourself

The most effective CV you'll ever write.
The best interview you'll ever give.
Secure the job you really want.

Second edition

Bill Faust and Michael Faust

PEARSON
Prentice Hall
BUSINESS

Harlow, England • London • New York • Boston • San Francisco • Toronto • Sydney • Tokyo • Singapore • Hong Kong
Seoul • Taipei • New Delhi • Cape Town • Madrid • Mexico City • Amsterdam • Munich • Paris • Milan

PEARSON EDUCATION LIMITED

Edinburgh Gate
Harlow CM20 2JE
Tel: +44 (0)1279 623623
Fax: +44 (0)1279 431059
Website: www.pearsoned.co.uk

First published in Great Britain in 2002
This second edition published 2006

ISBN: 978-0-273-70730-1

British Library Cataloguing in Publication Data
A CIP catalogue record for this book can be obtained from the British Library

Library of Congress Cataloging-in-Publication Data
A catalog record for this book is available from the Library of Congress

10 9 8 7 6 5 4
09 08 07

Typeset in 10pt Iowan Old Style by 70
Printed and bound in Great Britain by Ashford Colour Press Ltd, Gosport, Hants.

The publisher's policy is to use paper manufactured from sustainable forests.

Contents

Thank you from Michael and Bill

This book began when we asked ourselves whether the traditional CV could be improved. The answer was a resounding 'yes'. However, we did not set out to write a book but simply to improve our own career prospects.

We analyzed the traditional CV, identified a number of shortcomings and limitations. and developed some alternative ideas. These ideas were road-tested with a select group of people and they gave us generous advice and a positive thumbs-up response. One day, when talking with an executive-search firm, we were asked where we had discovered the Elevator Pitch and which book it came from. We then decided to develop our ideas further and share them with you. Without their initial acceptance of our ideas, without their feedback and without their questioning, this book would never have happened.

We would also like to thank our friends and colleagues who acted as sounding boards and were kind enough to let us use their life experiences. They acted as both judge and jury. Without them our words would be poorer. John Baldwin, Ken Livingstone, Justine Cobb, Mara Goldstein, Nancy Prendergast, Richard Davies, Jack Gratton, Mark Bailey, Charlie Dobres, Kate Marsh, Marc Schavemaker, Darren Fell, Louise Medley, Laura Neilson, Neil Howlin, Fiona Murie, Michael Matthews, David Shairp, Ana Molina, Erika Martin and Bert Zwiers.

We would also like to thank all the people who have supported us and encouraged us since the first edition was published. Special thanks must go to the careers management services at many of the leading global business schools and universities who have supported the ideas and concepts behind our approach and helped us make them more robust. They have been generous in their praise and time.

Thanks must also go to our publishing team at Pearson Education, Richard Stagg, Rachael Stock and their colleagues who helped us begin our journey. We'd also like to thank the international rights team for their help in making the book available in over 20 countries.

We would like to thank our partners and spouses. I'm eternally grateful for Kimi's perseverance, inspiration and gentle smile.

Bill would like to thank and dedicate this book to Jane and Daisy Mills and a special thanks to Sophie Baldwin.

We have now decided to update the first edition, first published in 2002, as our ideas have evolved based on all the generous input we've received.

We must finally thank you for purchasing our book. We hope you enjoy reading the second edition as much as we did creating it.

Thank you

Michael and Bill

Introduction

All you need to know, say and do

Pitch Yourself is the fresh and innovative way to sell yourself by getting your employer to buy you. To get the job you really want, you need to stand out from everyone else. At each step of the interview process you need to answer your next employer's one fundamental question, 'What do you offer me?' We call your answer to this fundamental question your Elevator Pitch. *Pitch Yourself* helps you:

➡ Create the most effective CV you'll ever write

➡ Give the best interview you'll ever give

➡ Write compelling cover letters

➡ Completely fill in application forms

➡ Manage assessment centres

➡ Manage your referees

You will learn how to communicate what makes you unique. You will understand what your potential employer is looking for. You will learn how to show them you have what they want at each step of the recruitment process. You'll transform the way you sell yourself through a radical and fundamental re-think of what makes you different.

Less than 30 seconds to impress

First impressions count. Your first contact with your next employer is crucial. If you don't make the right impression with your CV, with your cover letter, through an introductory meeting or perhaps in your first phone call with a search firm, it is too late. You'll never have that interview, you'll never be asked for references.

You have less then 30 seconds to make that first impression. Yes, less then 30 seconds. 20 to 30 seconds for a first pass scan of your CV. Less than 30 seconds to create the right impression. What are you going to write? Less than 30 seconds to travel five floors in an elevator? What are you going to say? Do you know how to use those seconds wisely? Can you sell yourself in less than 30 seconds? Can you use your 30 seconds to answer the only question that matters in the whole recruitment process, 'What will you do for me? What do you offer? What and where is your value add?' Less than 30 seconds to be selected. Less than 30 seconds to be de-selected. Surely you want to make sure your 30 seconds are the best they can be?

You'll learn how to communicate what makes you different in a compelling and succinct way. You'll learn how to make the most of your 30 seconds. You'll learn how to convert 30 seconds of selling into 30 seconds of buying. Your first impression will count.

Prepare once

You'll be taken through a step-by-step guide to help you understand what makes you different and unique. You will see the benefit of thorough preparation. You will be shown how to create a series of building blocks that are used to assemble your Elevator Pitch. The building blocks enable you easily to tailor and adapt your Elevator Pitch for each company. The building blocks make it easy to write a compelling cover letter, create a new CV, fill in application forms, prepare for assessment centres and win your interview.

You'll discover that your investment in time and energy saves you time later, ensures effective communication at each step, shortens the overall recruitment process and provides you with the best possible chance of securing your next job.

Correct preparation is fundamental to anything you do in life. This is especially true when you are looking for your next job. Your career is the fourth most important thing in the world after love, life and death. Do you want to leave your career to chance? Are you happy with an underperforming CV? Do you want a great cover letter or an insipid one? Do you want to ace that interview or just do okay? Wouldn't you love to maximize every chance you get? Wouldn't you like to be as prepared as you possibly could be? Do you want to perform to the best of your ability at every stage of the recruitment process? Are you happy to miss out on the job you really want?

Tested in the real world

Pitch Yourself has been widely acclaimed since it was first published in 2002.

The second edition has been revised and updated to incorporate feedback from our global seminar and lecture programme at over 40 leading business schools and universities across the world from MIT to Queens in North America, from RSM to the London Business School in Europe and from University of Otago to Macquarie Graduate School of Management, Sydney in Asia-Pac. As well as meeting the career advisors at these institutions, we've helped hundreds of people to implement our ideas and create their job-winning Elevator Pitches.

Your Elevator Pitch transforms the way you sell yourself to answer the most important question 'What do your offer me?' It realigns your focus from the past to the future and from the seller's perspective to the buyer's perspective. It makes the passive active. You prioritize who you are and how you work over what you were and where you've worked. Who you are and how you work are the qualities employers look for as they demonstrate your personality, your traits, your abilities, your future value and your potential performance in your new role.

You will be provided with the essential tools to create your own Elevator Pitch. You will learn how to discover and understand your traits, abilities and capabilities and emphasize what makes you stand out at every stage of the job process. You will see how to construct and write your own Elevator Pitch and how to position yourself in an over-crowded and over-communicated society.

Chapter 1 shows you why you need to stand out and why the traditional CV should be left to wither and die in the changing world of work.

Chapter 2 defines the building blocks of your Elevator Pitch; your Personal Promise, your Transferable Assets and your Career and Education Biography.

Chapter 3 tells you how to discover and create the building blocks of your own Elevator Pitch. A step-by-step practical guide walks you through the process. We'll show you what you need to know, say and do to create your building blocks.

Chapter 4 tells you how to assemble your Elevator Pitch using your building blocks to target and tailor each opportunity.

Chapter 5 is unusual and unique for a careers book. Here you will find real people who have been willing to share their experiences and their Elevator Pitches, from pilots to veterinary nurses to the Mayor of London.

Chapter 6 summarizes this unique approach. Help yourself today to get the best job tomorrow.

chapter

1

The death of the traditional CV

You will learn:

➡ Think and act differently

➡ The CV is dead

➡ Future performance not past performance

Think and act differently

Applying for a job is like going on a date. You wouldn't get anywhere if you simply made a list of everything you'd done. You need to create some excitement about yourself, your future and how that relates to your partner, before you have a chance of a relationship. You don't normally get married after one date and, like any relationship, getting your next job is about escalating expressions of desire.

How do you stand out from all the others who want the same job? Do you know the most important question you must ask yourself? Is a traditional CV good enough for your ambitions? Can you express your ideas about yourself in ways that speak directly to your interviewer's concerns and objectives? What are their concerns? Do you know yourself? Do you believe the key to being noticed is to communicate selectively? What is a cover letter meant to do? Do you feel that the interview is the start of a relationship? Do you want to get the job you

you must answer question your next 'What do you

really want? Is your career within your hands? Do you believe that changes in organizations impact the type of career you will have? Have you considered what makes a great CV different from an okay CV? When did you last take time out to find out? What is the most important question that has to be answered and when do you need to answer it?

The most important question

To get the job you want you must answer the most important question your next employer has, 'What do you offer me?'

You do this by getting under their skin, inhabiting their shoes, thinking like them and acting like them. You must think about their needs and how you can satisfy their needs. You need to imagine yourself on their side of the desk and ask whether you would buy you. You need to take into consideration the people who are filters, gatekeepers, influencers and buyers. You must understand what they take to be true as this defines what they look for and want.

You need to transform your relevant experience into hard evidence. You need to speak their language to create desire and interest. You need to clearly position why you are the one person for their role by

the most important employer has, offer me?'

articulating your achievements and how they relate to the job you're applying for. You will not tell people you are great but show them you are great.

You need to address and express yourself directly to their concerns and objectives with passion, commitment, poise and confidence. You need to sell yourself in a way that makes your employer want to buy you.

Answer the most important question all the time.

You answer your next employer's most important question the first time you can. The second time you can. The third time you can. You answer it every time you meet until they offer you a job. You answer it in different ways every time, but each time you speak directly to their concerns and objectives. As you don't get a second chance to make a first impression, the first time is the most important time.

How many times have you been disappointed at a presentation? You didn't gain a sense of purpose and direction right at the start. You quickly lost interest. The speaker seemed unsure of their content. They did not express the content clearly. They hadn't thought through what you wanted to know. Now think of the times you've interviewed people to join your team and reviewed their CVs. Did they put themselves in your shoes to make your job easier from the start?

Make your next employer buy you

Figure 1.1 represents a simplified recruitment process. Each step signifies an increased level of interest in hiring you from the cover letter to your offer. Each step in this relationship is about you. It's also about them and you need to find a way to engage quickly and consistently.

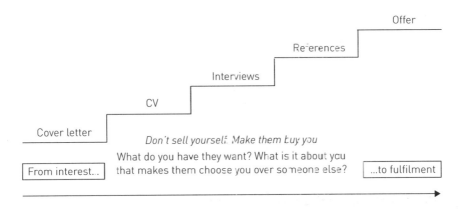

Figure 1.1 Show them you have what they want at each step

You'll meet gatekeepers, those who influence and those who decide. People will screen you out. You'll meet the search firm, the Human Resources Director, the Chief Executive, your next functional head, your prospective team members, your future colleagues or your competitors. You'll meet receptionists and secretaries. What impression do you want to leave with them? What are you selling?

Funky Business, a treatise on our new world order of funk, has this rallying cry:

> **"The moral: what companies sell and what their customers buy are two different things. Therefore, every once in a while it is wise to place yourself in the shoes of your customers and ask the question: 'What are they really buying?' The answer, 99 times out of 100, is not what you think you are selling"**
>
> *Funky Business*, J Ridderstrale and K. Nordstrom

Put yourself in their shoes and imagine trying to make the process as simple and as easy for them. Have you considered what's important for each of them to know and when they should know it? You need to think about their concerns, interests and values. If you're not sure what they are buying, can you answer their question, 'What do you offer me?'

You need to think concerns, interests

They're buying future performance

Competencies focus on how you do a job and the way you do it rather than what you do. They describe your underlying characteristics and traits that enable you to perform better in a role and go beyond the traditional focus of your qualifications.

Companies need the right people to do the right thing at the right time in the right place with the right tools. Competencies enable organizations to become more rigorous in their identification, analysis and evaluation of staff. Competencies have been developed, integrated and implemented by organizations to represent the language of performance as organizations flattened and management layers reduced. Figure 1.2 shows a company using competencies to provide a consistent analysis and evaluation methodology across time, geography, culture and work boundaries by creating a common vision and language across an organization – aligning the goals and behaviours of the business with the roles in the organization.

There is a link between the behaviours of the people in an organization and its corporate culture. This genetic code of the organization tends to be replicated in the way a company hires, promotes and develops its people and becomes stable over time. It defines a shorthand for how an organization thrives and who the organization believes it is. The

about their
and values

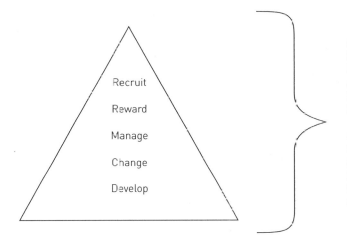

Figure 1.2   Competency integration

company's vision and mission define what an organization does. These three components of who, how and what define the Corporate Promise of an organization.

The company sets out the challenges it faces and the challenges relevant to each position. A job description is created integrating the actions and outcomes together with the behaviours that enable the person to meet and overcome the specific challenges. This job description is known as the Job DNA. A typical Job DNA might cover:

➡ Context: the context for the role from job dimensions to purpose.

➡ Need to do: what an individual needs to do from accountabilities to relationships.

➡ Need to know: the skills and knowledge and prior experience.

➡ Need to be: what the person needs to be from values, competencies to capabilities

Figure 1.3 shows the Corporate Promise and the Job DNA for your next employer. The competencies identified are specific to the role. The recruitment process, from interviews to references, looks at your past actions and actual behaviour in a specific situation in order to assess your match against the defined competencies.

Not all companies use competencies in such a rigorous manner. However, at every interview you have been to you will have been asked questions that are designed to uncover your competencies. You may

```
┌─────────────────────────┐
│                         │
│   Your Next Employer     │
│                         │
│                         │
│   Corporate Promise      │
│    Who. How. What        │
│                         │
│                         │
│       Job DNA            │
│     Competencies         │
│                         │
│                         │
│    Needs to Know         │
│     Needs to Do          │
│     Needs to Be          │
│                         │
│                         │
└─────────────────────────┘
```

Figure 1.3   Your next employer

not have realized it. They may not have realized it. Think back to some of the questions you have been asked and reflect on all the open-ended questions designed to test your thinking and how you solved the problem.

If they're buying competencies, what are you using to sell yourself? No doubt it's a traditional CV. Does it sell you? Would you buy you?

Your traditional CV is dead

The traditional CV is dead. Here's why.

Basic mistakes are made

A recent survey analyzed and evaluated 200 CVs submitted to a search firm and concluded:

→ Nearly one in three were considered poor as basic mistakes were made.

→ Roughly 4 out of 10 CVs had issues with structure and therefore understanding.

→ Nearly one quarter were over 3 pages long, putting undue pressure on the reader.

→ 34 percent of CVs could not easily and quickly answer what the person does and where have they done it.

→ 23 percent of CVs had evidence of incorrectly prioritizing less relevant information.

You might think this is a pretty sad state of affairs. You might also think the research conclusions are not an isolated example. You've experienced the same issues recruiting new people into your team. You've seen basic errors made as well as a lack of clarity on what the person would do for you. How many times did you read a list of personal qualities in a personal summary statement that bore no relationship to the rest of the CV? Ask yourself what the opposite would have said about that person? The five conclusions of the research can be collated into two broad themes. The first three conclusions concern presentation issues. The last two conclusions deal with the actual content of a CV posing the question 'What is the purpose of a CV?' Good content can be ruined by poor presentation though poor content will never be made good by good presentation.

The majority of CV books tell you to create an amazing CV by correcting the poor presentation. We disagree. There are fundamental issues with the content of a traditional CV.

Snapshot of the past

Your reverse chronological CV starts with your most recent role and implies that everything about your career was leading up to this point. It is historical and globally recognizable. As a catalogue, your traditional CV says what you did and where you did it. You have already been paid for this.

A traditional CV helps categorize you into silos that can be hard to break out of. This is especially true if you're changing function or

You can picture
CV as an

industry sector. A linear snapshot of the past is not the best tool to use as it emphasizes your last position which is no longer relevant to your future. Bill was pigeon-holed by search firms when he wished to move out of financial services yet remain in marketing. Despite a broad background in communication agencies managing a diverse range of businesses across a number of industry sectors and having worked in the marketing departments of international companies, he was seen only in the context of his last position.

Screens you out

The aim of the recruitment process is to minimize the risk of hiring rather than maximize the opportunity. Figure 1.4 illustrates the two typical two stages of any recruitment process. There is a need to screen candidates out to reduce the volume of potential people that can be seen and it is estimated that a first pass read of a CV takes 20 to 30 seconds. Screening is based on what are known as qualifiers – does your experience match what the company is looking for? – and is often narrowly focused on job title or industry. Screening is based on what you have done and where you have done it. Screening also tries to take into account what you might be able to do based on the experience you demonstrate on your CV. You can see that screening, the start of the recruitment process, focuses on your qualifications and experience yet these only tell a small part of your overall story. They do not get you

your traditional
iceberg

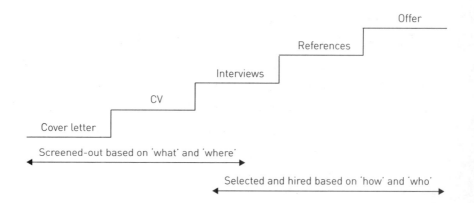

Figure 1.4 Minimizing risk

the job. They are your point of entry. There are three ways a traditional CV helps screen you out of opportunities: it doesn't talk their language; it needs to be deciphered; you look identical to others.

Doesn't talk their language

You can picture your traditional CV as an iceberg, much like Figure 1.5. There is substantially more of the iceberg below the water than above. The parts of the iceberg that are visible relate to what you did, the results you delivered, and where you did it. Substantial parts of the iceberg are under water. The hidden iceberg represents your competencies. Your competencies are those traits and behaviours that enabled you to deliver your results in the first place. They describe how you are able to deliver your results and who you are. Your traditional CV hides your competencies, your fundamental building blocks, behind a chronological and criteria-based façade. Your traditional CV does not talk the language of the person who'll hire you at each and every step of the recruitment process. Don't let your next job get shipwrecked on an iceberg of tradition and misinformation.

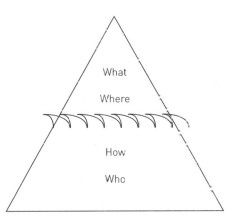

Figure 1.5   Your traditional CV iceberg

Needs deciphering

A traditional CV needs to be deciphered as you have not talked and used their language. Your next employer must unlock the criteria-based, functional and historical veneer of your CV to showcase your base motives, traits and competencies that enabled you to deliver the results in the first place. They need to unlock this veneer in a short 20 to 30 seconds for a first pass of your CV. You are letting someone decipher your CV, your Career DNA, your career genetic make-up, the most valuable thing you own, without providing them with a key. Deciphering is an inexact science. You're about to be de-selected based on a quick judgement using incorrectly prioritized information, written from your perspective, that is not focused on their needs.

Looks identical

Your traditional CV makes you look identical to the other candidates. All the CVs your next employer has in front of them show similar skills and experience. They find it hard to pick out a CV as they are unsure how you could help build them their organization or if you could thrive in their culture. Your personality is missing. They cannot see your style, your motivations or your values. You have made clear 'what' and 'where', which makes you look like everyone else, and you've missed out your 'who' and 'how', which are the key things that make you unique.

During a seminar at Edinburgh School of Management a lady said she'd just recruited a new doctor. She placed an advert in the press seeking someone with approximately 10 years' experience and a couple of specialist areas of expertise. She received over 100 CVs and each one satisfied the entry requirements. But nothing differentiated one CV from another. Asked how she could shortlist 6 to 8 doctors for interview, she replied it was done on personality by looking at their hobbies and interests! This could be a good way to select someone but the traditional CV had turned unique doctors into a homogeneous group. No-one stood out. Suppose one doctor had written about their competencies, which could have included identifying, organizing and planning resources, how they evaluate and interpret information, or how they work with others and comfortably deal with people from diverse backgrounds. They would have stood out. They might even have been a better doctor. The recruitment process would have been less haphazard.

Flexibility are key

No longer relevant

Over the last 100 years the CV became a standard world currency that is now debased by the changes in our work patterns and environments.

A traditional CV mirrors the traditional structure of a vertical career defined and delivered through a hierarchical organization. In turn this matches the structure of many recruitment agencies with their functional and industry silos set up to serve those organizations. A traditional CV drives the easiest fit not the best hire.

The fragmentation and erosion of traditional organizational structures change the way your career will evolve and change how you will be recruited and retained. The world will continue to be re-engineered, restructured, merged, consolidated, networked, matrixed, downsized and delayered. Thinner and flatter organizations have emerged to replace the formal ties of hierarchy, functional specialists and job titles. These organizational models place greater emphasis on decentralized cross-functional teams in networked relationships working across a flexible matrix, with individuals having knowledge and taking action. Flexibility and agility are key dynamics. Multiple skills are required to navigate around. Loyalty to the company declines as individuals own their new and increasingly horizontal careers. Career patterns, the nature and scope of management, leadership and the skills and abilities required for the future are evolving. There is greater autonomy and

and agility
dynamics

fewer directives. Emphasis is placed on the need to learn and adapt rather than perform and execute. Authority is no longer conferred by title but earned by respect.

It is no longer feasible to believe that your past, defined by what you did and where you did it, is a barometer of your future worth. Linearity is dead. Your traditional CV belongs to the days of those obsolete corporate monoliths that are crumbling and changing around you. Your traditional CV is a strait-jacket on your ability to successfully sell yourself in this new world of work.

Future performance not past performance

If people are looking for you to demonstrate your competencies in the recruitment process, you shouldn't make them work too hard.

Figure 1.6 shows how you should respond to the change in the way companies hire and recruit by adapting to their way of thinking. There's no reason to live in the past hiding beneath the façade of a traditional CV, emphasizing your past performance as it helps screen you out. It does not answer your next employer's key question: 'What do you offer me?'

The world has moved on and it is time to focus on your future performance. Competencies are the language of future performance

Competencies are future

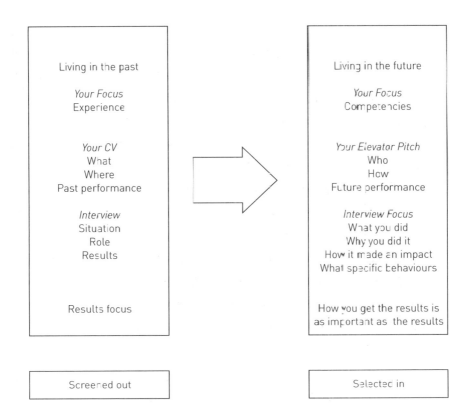

Figure 1.6 Living with competencies

and prove to your next employer how you did it, what you did, and why you did it. Competencies help them to understand your future capability in a non-linear dynamic world. Competency frameworks are

the language of performance

embedded and integrated into organizations to frame their recruitment, development and retention policies. Competencies are normally used to assess and evaluate people once they are in the recruitment funnel but not explicitly at the start of the funnel. Research has proven that you can improve your chance to be selected, which is the critical start of any job process, by demonstrating your competencies at this stage. You improve your chance of being short-listed if you include competency statements at the application stage. Bright and Earl, two Australian organizational psychologists, who consult and write on career development, selection, testing and training, researched the inclusion and exclusion of competency state-ments and how these impacted the decision by recruiters to shortlist a candidate. The results were consistent and they concluded that 'the more competency statements you put in . . . the more chance you have of being shortlisted.'

You should demonstrate your competencies at all steps of the recruitment process as they make a real difference and improve the chances of getting the job you really want.

'Who' and 'how' is now more important than 'what' and 'where'.

chapter

2

The Elevator Pitch

You will learn:

➡ The purpose of each step in the recruitment process

➡ To define the building blocks of your Elevator Pitch

The purpose of each step in the recruitment process

Six floors of separation

As you step into a lift you spot the Chief Executive or the Human Resources Director of the company you'd love to work for heading towards you. They get into the lift. They just happen to be in this building, in this city, in this part of the world at the same time as you. The top floor button is pushed. You have a captive audience. You have six floors, or about 60 seconds, to open a conversation and excite them about how you could help their organization. You're reminded of the film *Casablanca* when Bogart says 'Of all the gin joints in all the towns in all the world she walks into mine' or perhaps you're feeling more upbeat and think of Forrest Gump, 'My momma said life was like a box of chocolates . . . you never know what you're gonna get.'

You've just wasted some valuable time. You've only five floors left. Now you have just four floors left. What are you going to do? Can you

Who is
from you

take advantage of this serendipity and destiny? What are you going to say? Can you summarize yourself in a way that is meaningful to them in the next 30 seconds? Maybe you would say nothing as you were afraid of blowing your chances?

This might sound fanciful but Otis, who have roughly 28 percent share of the world's new elevator equipment market, estimate that elevators carry the equivalent of the world's population every 72 hours. That's roughly 6.4 billion people every 72 hours! How many chance conversations could you have? Perhaps your chance will come the next time you step into a lift?

Six floors kept you from your goal, just six floors of separation. You may have heard that everyone on Earth is separated from anyone else by no more than six degrees of separation. You can be connected to any other person on the planet through a chain of acquaintances that has no more than five intermediaries. You could meet anyone you wanted to. Who do your colleagues and friends know that you'd like to meet? What about the person who is standing next to you in the lunch queue? At the bus stop? Who is six degrees from you right now? If you were to meet, what would the person making the advocated introduction say about you? What would you tell them to say about you? How could you get that meeting? Are you ready for your serendipity? Are you ready for your conversation?

six degrees right now?

Are you ready for your conversation?

Your Elevator Pitch is the most compelling thing you could say, write or do that proves to someone you have what they want. Your Elevator Pitch focuses on how you are going to help your employer and is designed to get you noticed. Think of yourself as a collection of competencies that can be bundled together in different ways. You get noticed when you effectively develop, bundle, market and sell your competencies.

Figure 2.1 illustrates the process of finding a new job. The left-hand side of the diagram represents your job-hunting strategy. You've examined the external environment, the market and industry, to

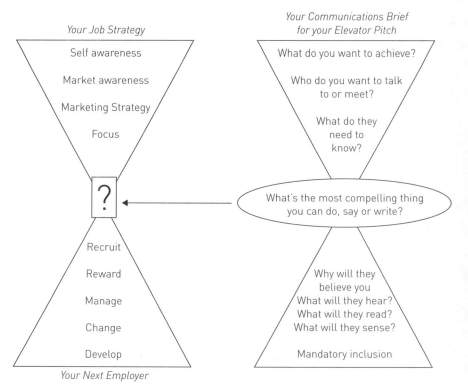

Figure 2.1 Meeting their needs

identify what you might choose to do. You've examined your internal environment, by gaining greater self-understanding, and determined what you can do based on your discovery and bundling of your competencies. This identifies the company you could work for and the job you'd like to do represented by their recruitment and development funnel in the bottom left triangle. The right-hand side of Figure 2.1 represents the communications brief necessary to deliver your chosen strategy and create your Elevator Pitch. It shows the questions you answer to ensure your communication is focused on the right person at the right time saying the right thing in the right way. The most motivating and compelling thing you could say, write or do to make them hire you is answered when you meet their needs in an exciting and relevant way.

To develop the compelling message that gets you noticed and secures the job you want, you must understand both the company and yourself. You understand yourself and understand your value when you identify, analyze, evaluate and innovatively bundle your competencies which, in turn, determines how you meet their needs. Whilst talking at some of the business schools and universities, we sometimes ask if anyone would like to come to the front and talk about themselves for two minutes. People often find excuses by thinking 'Oh, I'm not very good at this.' If we had asked them to spend two minutes talking on their hobby or favourite sport it would've been a different story. This doesn't make much sense. Why do you feel more comfortable talking about your favourite sport than about yourself? If you don't understand yourself how can you tell others what you do or why they should employ you?

The way in which your Elevator Pitch is remembered is important. If your Elevator Pitch is remembered then *you* are remembered.

"You need to leave the reader with an impression of you in their mind. According to the 'Constructivist' theory of memory, proposed by the theorists Bartlett and Ebbinghaus, the way a person remembers you will depend on what is in that person's mind already. So you will need to create your Elevator Pitch in ways that connect with the person who is reading it or listening to you."

Dr Harri Burgess, UK psychologist

To do this, imagine you are that person. Imagine their likely working life and interests. Try to find a commonality between you and them and be sure to incorporate it into your Elevator Pitch. The reader of your Elevator Pitch, or your interviewer, is more likely to remember you if the image you create of yourself has a connection to an area of their own interest – even if it's not directly relevant to the job. To prove the above point, you can practise this exercise with a good friend. Write a two-paragraph, detailed account on a topic of interest to you (a hobby or sport for example, and be sure to put in lots of detail). Then ask a friend to read it twice, put it to one side and recall it 15 minutes later. You are likely to find your friend remembers the account in much more detail if it is something they already have encountered in their life. In contrast, they will find something obscure difficult to recall in detail. It is highly likely you will also find they have embellished and added new detail to it! This is evidence that the information you have given has been linked, in their brains, to the memories they already had.

Your Elevator
30 second

One of the key ways your Elevator Pitch will make the right connections and links with the person reading, or listening to you, is to craft it from their perspective and uses their language, the language of competencies, in a consistent way. You focus their attention on the things you have that they want, to maximize each and every step of the recruitment process, as shown in Figure 2.2. Your Elevator Pitch is a 30 second conversation. It's the twenty-first century CV with a power and force that can be extracted and distilled in 20–30 seconds of first reading. It is a brief for you to prepare for interviews. Your Elevator Pitch briefs and informs your referees.

Your communication needs differ with each step of the recruitment process. Good communication reflects the intelligence, the time and

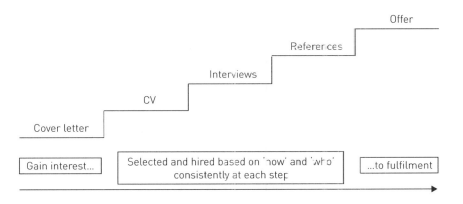

Figure 2.2 Employed for 'who' and 'how'

Pitch is a conversation

the needs of the other party. Figure 2.3 shows the role of your cover letter is to get your CV read. The role of your CV is to get an interview. The role of your application form is to get an interview. The role of your interview is to get an offer. The role of attending an assessment centre is to get an offer. The role of your referees is to confirm their findings.

Your cover letter tells your next employer how you meet their corporate requirements. Your CV or application form evidences how you meet the job requirements. Your interview proves how you meet the job requirements. An assessment centre demonstrates across a number of tasks how you meet the job requirements. Your referees confirm that they and their colleagues observed and acknowledged that what you said is true.

With each step, your new employer gains deeper and cumulative knowledge about you.

Steps	Your Purpose	How
Cover letter	Read my CV	Tell
CV or Application form	Negative: Don't screen me out Positive: Interview me	Evidence
Interviews 1-n	Get the offer	Prove
Assessment centres	Get the offer	Demonstrate
References	Confirm	Confirm

Figure 2.3 Who needs to know what and by when

Defining the building blocks of your Elevator Pitch

There are three building blocks to your Elevator Pitch. Each building block is made up of smaller building blocks. Everything has been designed to be assembled together to help you at each stage of the recruitment process from creating a killer CV, briefing referees, writing cover letters, interview preparation, assessment centres, to application forms. The three core building blocks are:

➡ Your Personal Promise

➡ Your Transferable Assets stored as an inventory in your Career DNA Bank

➡ Your Career and Education Biography

Your Elevator Pitch is founded on your Transferable Assets. A Transferable Asset is a competency you can demonstrate using at the same level of complexity across multiple situations. Your Career DNA Bank is an inventory of your Transferable Assets representing your genetic career code. Your Personal Promise is an executive summary that summarizes the benefit of your Transferable Assets. This framework is designed to bundle and focus the source of value, your Transferable Assets, as unique and authentic benefits to your next employer.

Personal Promise

The Personal Promise has been designed to solve the problem endemic to the personal summaries you find at the top of many traditional CVs. Normally this is a list of subjective adjectives eliciting the 'so what?' response as they weren't substantiated and proven by the later contents of the traditional CV. They are created without authenticity and objectivity as they are not founded in reality. Did anyone ever stop and ask 'What would the reverse say about me? Who wouldn't want to be customer focused? Or hard-working?' The issue with a personal summary has been the execution not the concept.

You will notice that we have changed the name from a personal summary to a Personal Promise. One looks ahead, one looks back. A Personal Promise is a guarantee of future performance. Your Personal Promise helps create a three-dimensional picture enabling your next employer to immediately grasp the three key benefits you bring:

➡ Who you are

➡ How you do it

➡ What you do

Your Personal Promise clearly signposts what you offer and why someone should continue to read on or why they should continue to listen to you by making the relevant links and connections. You tell them you have what they want and introduce your personal qualities at each stage of the recruitment process.

Below are a few of the Personal Promises that are explored later in the book.

Your Personal
signposts what

"I bring zest for life to my work. I find solutions by understanding which questions need to be asked. 18 years of practical, integrated marketing ideas generation in wide-ranging industry sectors from advertising to publishing throughout the world."

"I have a calm and considered approach to my life. A qualified veterinary nurse of 11 years. If I could, I would ride my horse to work."

"Intelligent risk taker. Direction setter of inventive solutions with the willingness to absorb situations and get on with it. 28 years' leadership of $ multimillion mechanical engineering projects in the international oil industry."

Your Personal Promise should be like the ones above – direct, simple, clear and directional. It should be *you*.

"When I look at traditional CVs, I rarely see the true candidate underneath. I love the Personal Promise – it reveals the hidden personality and brings life to the Elevator Pitch. We can often forget that personal attributes are tremendous selling points at interview: The Personal Promise showcases them at the application stage."

Alison Edmonds: Director CMS Manchester Business School UK

Promise clearly you offer

Transferable Assets and Career DNA Bank

Transferable Assets are your fiduciary currency. Just as a bank note promises to pay the bearer a certain sum in the future, your Transferable Assets are your tokens that guarantee the promise of your future contribution and value.

Transferable Assets are the source of your value and competitive advantage. A Transferable Asset is a competency you can evidence by demonstrating its use at the same level of complexity across multiple situations. A competency focuses on how you do a job and the way you do it rather than on what you do. Your results demonstrate your level of capability in a competency.

Competencies represent the language of performance. A competency is what you must be able to do to deliver the desired results of your role. Competencies are the behaviours or cluster of behaviours that relate to the way things are done. They describe the underlying characteristics and traits that enable you to perform better in your role and go beyond the traditional focus of your qualifications, technical skills and experience. Competencies are specific and behavioural. They are observable and measurable. You are capable of developing more competencies and developing existing competencies in greater depth.

Competencies
a job is done
what is

Competencies are specific to the company and a role. Competencies can be business or technical in nature. Business competencies can be split into either threshold or performance competencies. Threshold competencies, such as integrity and trust, are the key behaviours that you need to demonstrate regardless of your function and seniority but they do not necessarily differentiate performance. Performance competencies such as customer focus, developing direct reports or learning on the fly, are those behaviours that distinguish excellent from average performance. Technical competencies are unique to your function and are the behaviours that ensure success within the function such as marketing or accounting. Competencies can be singular in nature, such as perseverance. Competencies can also be made up of a number of singular competencies or smaller groupings. An example might be visionary leadership and creating buy-in, which could be components of a higher competency such as envision.

Competencies focus on how a job is done rather than on what is done. Figure 2.4 illustrates that the results you achieve are underpinned by the associated competencies. Competencies are an extension of your knowledge, skills and abilities. Skills and abilities are the basic nuts and bolts of a competency and are things like judgement or reading through to a physical attribute such as increased lung capacity for a

focus on *how* rather than on done

world class cyclist or rower. Knowledge is passive information on a subject, such as accounting. Personality trait is a tendency to behave in a certain way, such as flexibility. Just because you have some knowledge, skills and abilities does not mean you will exhibit that competency. However, to have the competency you must have a combination of the associated knowledge, skills and abilities and be combining them and using them in the correct way. You cannot be competent if you don't know, or don't know how to, use the building blocks of the competency.

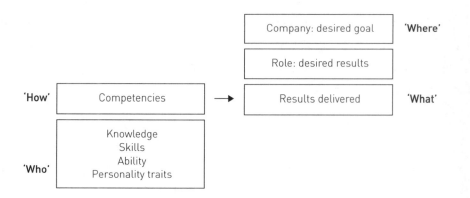

Figure 2.4 The competency mix

It is the level of behaviour of a competency and not its mere presence or absence that drives performance. Competencies are normally broken down into four or five cumulative levels of complexity, as seen in Figure 2.5. As the level of complexity increases, the type of behaviours change that indicate demonstration of this behaviour at this level. As the complexity level of the competency increases, what you need to know, the skills you need to have, the abilities you need to develop, and the personality traits you need to exhibit increase.

Competency: Adaptability

Definition: Adapting in order to work effectively in ambiguous or changing situations, and with diverse individuals and groups.
[Scale progression: more proactive, greater ambiguity/change]

Level 1 Recognizes the need to adapt	Level 2 Adapts to the situation	Level 3 Adapts to widely varied needs	Level 4 Adapts plans and goals	Level 5 Adapts organizational strategies
• Expresses willingness to do things differently. • Understands and recognizes the value of other points of view and ways of doing things. • Displays a positive attitude in the face of ambiguity and change.	• Changes own behaviour or approach to suit the situation. • Flexibly applies rules or procedures, while remaining guided by the organization's values. • Adapts behaviour to perform effectively under changing or unclear conditions.	• Adapts to new ideas and initiatives across a wide variety of issues or situations. • Supports and adapts to major changes that challenge traditional ways of operating. • Adapts interpersonal style to highly diverse individuals and groups in a range of situations. • Anticipates change and adapts own plans and priorities accordingly.	• Adapts organizational or project plans to meet new demands and priorities. • Revises project goals when circumstances demand it. • Recognizes and responds quickly to shifting opportunities and risks.	• Adjusts broad/macro organizational strategies, directions, priorities, structures and processes to changing needs in the environment. • Adapts behaviour to perform effectively amidst continuous change, ambiguity and, at times, apparent chaos. • Shifts readily between dealing with macro strategic issues and critical details. • Anticipates and capitalizes on emerging opportunities and risks.

Copyright 2005, Human Resource Systems Ltd. [www.hrsg.ca]

Figure 2.5 A sample competency definition

A competency has been defined. Your capability in that competency has been defined by the level of complexity at which you demonstrate that competency. Your competency is transformed into your Transferable Asset when you demonstrate its use at the same level of complexity across a wide range of situations. You cannot have a Transferable Asset if you have only demonstrated the use of a competency a couple of times. You will need to draw on your experiences at several different companies, and in several different roles in order to evidence your Transferable Assets. Like any tool that measures performance, any statements used to demonstrate and evidence your Transferable Assets requires substantiation. You must quantify the quality of your Transferable Assets. Achievements should be specific and timely: achieved Z by doing Y resulting in X within time T. Increased profit by 15 percent by increasing customer loyalty adding £5 million to bottom line in less than 12 months.

It might help to think of the Formula One season. What is a possible competency for a Formula One driver? Some of the requisite knowledge, skills and abilities could include:

➡ Knowledge of different circuits and weather conditions

➡ Knowledge of car dynamics and engineering – how late can one brake when entering a corner to the effect of different tyres

➡ Driving

➡ Spatial awareness

➡ Fast reaction times, hand–eye–feet coordination

➡ Physical strength and endurance

➡ Inner game – the desire to win

Part of the overall Formula One driver competency could be to develop a Formula One car capable of consistently winning Formula One races by zeroing in on the critical few points from all the information constantly received, such as car performance, and to communicate this back to the pit instantly, after the race and at testing intervals to further develop the car. This could be extended to include adapting to different conditions on a race circuit and racing effectively and consistently on different circuits or remaining calm under pressure.

Michael Schumacher clearly does this better, faster, more comprehensively and more consistently than many other Formula One drivers otherwise he wouldn't win as often or make pole position as often. By 2005 he had held the Driver's Championship title five times.

Your Career DNA Bank is an inventory of your Transferable Assets representing your genetic career code, your Career DNA. Your career DNA is unique and identifiable, indicating how well you perform compared to others. Unlike biological DNA, your Career DNA expands as you experience new roles, dynamics, cultures, events and tasks within the workplace and social environment. You should think of your Career DNA Bank as a heterogeneous collection of Transferable Assets that can be bundled together in a variety of ways to create your market position.

You know you should tailor every approach made to a potential employer, though many of us don't, as it takes time and is laborious. Your Career DNA Bank simplifies the adaptation and tailoring process. You select the most pertinent Transferable Assets from your extended inventory in your Career DNA Bank to suit the project you're facing and select the best examples that demonstrate each Transferable Asset. This is similar to your own biological DNA, when certain parts of the

Your Career DNA experience new cultures, events

genetic code are switched on and other parts switched off to form specialized cells most suited to the task in hand.

"The concepts of Transferable Assets and competencies are so on-target that each member of the team has been given a copy of *Pitch Yourself* to use as a tool in their student resumé coaching. Our MBA students who have used *Pitch Yourself* as a resumé guide have found it to be 100% useful in their resume preparation."

Jackie Wilbur, Director of Programmes: MIT Sloan School of Management US

Career and Education Biography

You should create a table that has the following columns:

→ Company name

→ Dates you worked for them

→ Short description of the company

→ Job title

→ Job dimensions

→ Responsibilities

→ Benefit of your job

expands as you roles, dynamics, and tasks

→ Education, graduate and postgraduate degrees and honours attained

Turning fact into evidence

Your Elevator Pitch is based on hard evidence rather than hard facts. Facts are pieces of information divorced from their context. You can apply the 'so what' test to facts. Evidence is a fact that has been given context, which makes it more likely to be understood and remembered by the person reading your Elevator Pitch or listening to you in the interview. Your Personal Promise is evidenced by your Transferable Assets. Your Transferable Assets are evidenced by demonstrating their use at the same level of complexity across multiple situations. Your Career and Educational Biography further evidences what you say.

The building blocks of your Elevator Pitch are now defined as shown in Figure 2.6. The next chapter helps you discover and create your own building blocks.

**Your Elevator Pitch
building blocks:**

Personal Promise
Who. How. What

Career DNA Bank
Transferable Assets

Knowledge
Skills
Abilities
Personality

Career and Education Biography
Benefit of your role

Figure 2.6   Your Elevator Pitch building blocks

chapter

3

Create the
building blocks

You will learn

➡ How to create the building blocks of your Elevator Pitch

How to create the building blocks of your Elevator Pitch

Creating the building blocks of your Elevator Pitch helps unlock new insights, helps you to see things more clearly, and is the key step that underpins the development of your Elevator Pitch. Time and effort need to be focused on building the correct foundations. There are three core blocks: your Personal Promise, a Career DNA Bank of Transferable Assets, and your Career Biography. It is best to begin with the Career DNA Bank.

Your Transferable Assets and Career DNA Bank

Your Career DNA Bank is an inventory of your Transferable Assets. A Transferable Asset is a competency you can evidence by demonstrating its use at the same level of complexity across multiple situations.

Your Career DNA Bank is like a bank account and your Transferable Assets the currency. You fill your bank account by identifying each of

Your Career DNA bank account and Assets the

your unique Transferable Assets. As you experience new roles, dynamics, cultures, events and tasks within the workplace and social environment, your Career DNA Bank will grow as you develop new Transferable Assets or develop an existing Transferable Asset in greater depth.

There are three cumulative steps to identify and evidence your Transferable Assets:

1 Develop a list of possible competencies, knowledge, abilities and skills by deconstructing your career, project by project, task by task.

2 Identify and evidence your competencies by looking for common groupings of competencies.

3 Identify and evidence your Transferable Assets by looking for common use of evidenced competencies

Step 1 Develop list of possible competencies: deconstruct your career

Step 1 is to develop a list of possible competencies, knowledge, abilities and skills by deconstructing your career, project by project, task by task, using the Objective–Analysis–Action–Results (OAAR)

bank is like a your Transferable currency

methodology. This enables you to construct a simple yet tight narrative of each and every aspect of your work, social and education life which is then used and expanded upon in Steps 2 and 3.

➡ **The Objective** sets out the task you had to deliver

➡ **The Analysis** phase looks at your thinking and evaluation of the options you had to deliver the task

➡ **The Action** phase is the implementation of your chosen options.

➡ **The Results** are the outcomes of your actions

Let's consider a relatively simple OAAR analysis case created by a veterinary nurse.

Case study: Veterinary Nurse's OAAR

Objective: To lead and ensure the smooth running of a team of seven nurses in a busy mixed country practice.

Analysis: Benchmark similar practices around the country. Looked at record for previous two years' vet practice management (who does what, where and why) and discovered seasonal trend. Productivity and efficiency compromised.

Action: Developed new staff rotas to take advantage of trend to free staff to concentrate on their core responsibilities and not be diverted onto unproductive tasks. Held meetings to explain rationale and expected benefit.

Result: Freed up additional 20 hours a month of time for every four employees ensuring vets could be vets and nurses could nurse. Greater efficiency and savings made as nursing staff were available for theatre, consulting, laboratory, hospitalized patients, practice administration including small-animal claim forms, nursing rotas and on-call out-of-hour duties. Made time available for practice nurses and resources for the dispensing of drugs and the teaching of student nurses.

The OAAR case study for the veterinary nurse could have been split into a number of smaller sub-objectives. However, the work was fairly straightforward. With more complex situations objectives often need to be broken down into smaller objectives. Your analysis highlights a number of options. You choose which options will be taken forward as actions. Some of the actions will be focused on directly fulfilling the original objective. Some of the actions are focused on the intermediary steps necessary to fulfil the original objective. These actions become new objectives. These new objectives spark a new cycle of OAARs.

It is likely you will find several new objectives resulting from the initial analysis, action phase as shown in Figure 3.1 The idea is to break

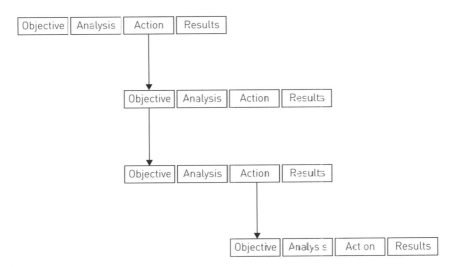

Figure 3.1   Unpacking the Russian doll

down your composite objective into the smallest units possible. If your objective was to achieve a 10% growth in market share within 12 months in order to grow faster than the market what were all of your other OAAR sub-routines that enabled you to do that? You should also go through the same process for both your academic life and your hobbies and interests. It may help if you to liken this exercise to undoing a 'Russian doll'. Opening one doll reveals the next smaller doll. Opening that doll reveals the next smaller doll. Each new doll you expose takes you deeper into your analysis and actions and results that enabled you to deliver your core objective. You need to repeat the process again and again until you have reduced your career into its smallest OAAR chunks.

A senior executive from the software industry broke down her objective into several smaller micro-objectives. Her composite objective was to increase productivity by X% by developing a process to increase quality control within 12 months. In the analysis phase of her first OAAR she considered the resources available and concluded that a new team was needed. Her action point in her first OAAR was to recruit and develop a new team. This then became a new objective

You need to peel
unpack the
and get under

and the start of another OAAR analysis, which in turn led to an analysis of the functional specification of the new department including head count, job specifications, set-up and running costs to resource allocation. The action was to recruit the team against agreed headcount and budget. At the same time, arising from the original analysis–action phase, she also knew a further micro-objective was to create a new software-testing capability and this became another OAAR piece of analysis. Throughout the project she was involved in stakeholder governance, selling the plans to the Board and other department heads in order to integrate the new department into the organization. She also created a series of OAARs covering areas such as managing upwards to the Board, to the identification and negoti-ation of third party suppliers.

You need to peel back the layers, unpack the Russian doll, and get under your skin. Breaking down a composite objective into its singular components takes time and honesty. We have included a list of questions that may help you as you go through your OAAR analysis.

back the layers, Russian doll, your skin

Breaking down your OAAR

Your Objective

➡ What objectives are on your job specification?

➡ If your boss were sitting here now, what would they say you did or did not do?

➡ What stepping stones were you aware you needed? How did you know? How did you break the objective down?

➡ What did your company, department or team have or do that it did not want to have or do in the future? When was this?

➡ What didn't the company, department or team have or do that it wanted to have or do in the future? When was this?

➡ What was the expected result? Who would benefit? By when? By how much?

➡ What was measured and with reference to what external norm?

Your Analysis

➡ What did you know? What didn't you know? What would you have liked to know?

➡ What would or wouldn't have happened if you had made this change? What would or wouldn't have happened if you had not made this change?

➡ What did you do? In what order? What were the dependencies?

➡ Anything else?

➡ Did you need to include further stepping stones?

➡ What did you learn?

➡ What internal and external resources did you need?

➡ Who did you consult and agree the analysis with?

The Action

➡ What did you implement?

➡ How did you implement?

➡ When did you implement?

➡ What part did you play?

The Result

➡ What was the result?

➡ Who benefited?

➡ How much did they benefit?

➡ When did they benefit?

➡ How was the benefit qualified and quantified?

➡ What benchmark or norm was used to agree the benefit?

➡ Who or what decided that the result was a success or not?

➡ If you take yourself to the point of time when you had achieved the objectives what are you hearing? What do you see? What are you feeling? What are you saying to yourself? What was the organization saying to itself?

We suggest you download your conscious brain quickly. Commit your OAAR analyses to a piece of paper. You may find it helpful to transfer the key learnings to a simple OAAR table. This process is about you. You must consider your level of involvement in the objective, in the analysis, with the action and your accountability for the results. What bit did you do? Did you consult, facilitate or liaise? Design, develop, or implement? Did you assist, manage or lead? Change, clarify, compose, collaborate, contribute, construct, or counsel? Did you decrease, direct, devise, divest? Did you eliminate, enter, examine, extract? Did you envision, engage or execute?

What bit did consult, facilitate

An exercise that might help you with the process of creating your OAARs is to think of your career as a timeline. Imagine a line representing your career with your past career on one side and your future career on the other. Step onto your timeline. Walk down your timeline towards your last company. Stop and think of the main events for you within that company, such as a promotion or something you were proud of. Look around you. What do you think, feel or see? What would you like to pick up? What is of value in your future? Look around you now. What did you do? More importantly, how did you do it and what enabled you to do it? What lessons did you learn? What happened? Pick up all those good things. You'll want the best bits of your past to help in your future career. In your future you'll be paid for how you do things and how you can do it again. Have you picked up all of your hows? Walk down your career timeline to all the places you have worked. Now imagine walking to the present day and looking along your future career timeline. Walk to where you feel comfortable. Have you got what you need?

You shouldn't confine your thinking to examples from work. What about your last holiday? You've been diving on the Great Barrier Reef in Australia and a Great White attacked you. You're in the pub with your friends and they want to know how you escaped. You don't spare the gory details as you explain your first thought when you saw the

you do? Did you or liaise?

shark beneath you, how you outwitted the shark, how you avoided becoming lunch, how you managed to get back onto the dive boat and your relief when you realized you were safe. This story, if true, would certainly make your friends think you're calm and resourceful under great stress; it might reinforce their belief that you can handle a crisis. They'd also know you had a large dose of true grit, determination and courage. What have you done in your personal life?

You have now generated tens, if not hundreds, of individual OAAR examples as you pulled apart your Russian doll. To provide some additional context and content, look back at your performance appraisals or your 360 feedback reviews and see what they can tell you. There are two things you must do before you move on to step 2.

First, check the language you've used. As you read each of your OAARs you should convert any passive sentences into active statements. Active statements begin with a verb such as analyzed, managed or designed. Ensure your active statements are specific as you want clarity and brevity. You want a tight objective: delivered X by doing Y achieving Z by time T. This objective is mirrored by a tight result: Achieved Z by doing Y within time T resulting in X. All the statements should be written in the third person.

What have you personal

Second, look for common areas of strengths and weaknesses. What do I do well? What don't I do well? What do I need to keep doing? What do I need to stop doing? How do I do well? How do I do badly? What did I learn? Commit your answers to a piece of paper.

Step 2 **Identify and evidence your competencies**

Step 2 identifies and evidences your competencies by grouping your OAARs based on how you used and combined your knowledge, skills and abilities to deliver the results. Figure 3.2 shows how the OAAR analysis is used to help identify and evaluate your competencies. Your Objective tells you what you wanted to do. The Analysis and Action sections provide the clues to your behaviour patterns and competencies. These sections answer how you do things with the clear and direct inference that you can do it again. The Result answers what you did.

Take the Analysis and Action sections of each OAAR and search for those competencies you believe you demonstrated in order to achieve the objective. At this stage you can describe the competency in many ways. You can also include as many competencies as you want. Let's consider three examples.

done in your life?

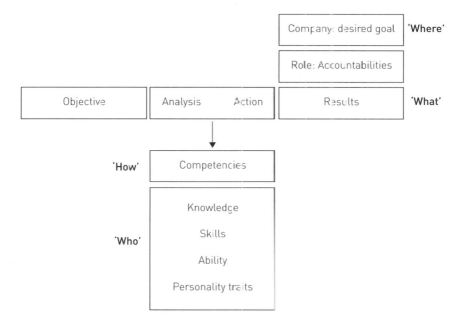

Figure 3.2 Understanding your OAAR analysis

First, let's return to the senior executive in the software industry where she had identified an objective to recruit a new team and created an OAAR for that piece of work. From her OAAR analysis she knew she had recruited and blended people into a team creating a shared purpose and the team was quickly accepted and integrated into the company. This manifested itself in being able to build a new system from scratch and on time to deliver the agreed productivity increases. The competency she demonstrated was building effective teams. In addition she can evidence several competencies from her main composite objective. These could range from planning the way forward, which is essentially an ability to plan realistically, organize resources to deliver tasks and review what needs to happen by when. She could also use commercial awareness by focusing on how the relevant information was used to achieve the objective and how the new department impacted the bottom line.

Second, let's consider an example from Bill's career when he was working for an Australian advertising agency and responsible for generating new business opportunities. One of the leading newspaper groups approached the agency with a brief to strengthen their customer service through improving the relationship between their sales force and their client counterparts by providing accurate, up-to-the-minute information to their sales teams regardless of the Australian time zones. Bill's task was to win the business. This OAAR is slightly unusual. The advertising agency has an objective. The prospective client has an objective. The agency objective can only be fulfilled if the client objective is fulfilled. In an ideal world each would be separated out and treated as a separate OAAR analysis.

Case study: Marketing Consultant's OAAR

Objective
- ➡ *Agency objective:* Win the business by demonstrating empathy with the prospective client.
- ➡ *Client brief:* Improve media rates and the amount of advertising space sold by providing the sales teams with the ability to supply

their clients with up-to-date information of the rates and media space availability regardless of location and time zones.

Analysis

➡ Analyzed the market and the publisher–media agency relationships.

➡ Identified a number of new customers to those specified in the original brief.

➡ Set up a project team and managed the internal agency resources to create and develop the proposal.

➡ Gained agreement internally to the proposal through the agency quality management process for new business pitches.

Action

➡ Created and presented a simple and cost-effective strategy to build an interlinked intranet, internet and extranet to distribute the real time data (sharing of common files), irrespective of geography and time zone over Asia-Pac, to the newspapers sales force as well as customized real-time information to all of their existing and potential customers (the media buyers).

Result

➡ Fairfax would gain the best rates possible for their media space, potentially revolutionizing the media planner buyer and publisher relationship for the better.

➡ Their clients receive information that was accurate and would differentiate them from their main competitors.

➡ Agency won business.

Bill can identify a number of competencies from this OAAR: team management, provider of innovative solutions, creating buy-in, understanding commercial imperatives, ability to see the big picture; clear oral and written communication skills.

Last is an example from Michael when he was at Dell. His remit was to develop and implement the Dell EMEA brand strategy within the global context to strengthen the affinity, commitment and preference for the Dell EMEA brand suite and support the business segment goals. One of the objectives necessary to fulfil the main objective was to adapt and launch the new global television and print campaign across Europe, supporting key territories at sufficient levels of activity within a given budget and time to affect changes in Dell's knowledge, preference and consideration sets. The analysis discovered that the three pillars of the objective could not be delivered simultaneously and a choice was required on whether a pillar was reduced in scope, countries and results, or increased in scope, budget and time. Rather than seek a budget increase a new objective was set.

Case study: Brand Strategist's OAAR

Objective
  ⇒ Step-change the budget by looking outside the normal funding arena and develop new models of participation at zero cost to Dell.

Analysis
  ⇒ Identified and evaluated alternative funding sources.

Action
  ⇒ Conceived and negotiated series of back-to-back interlocking deals with partners from the worlds of media, sport and IT.

Result

➡ Delivered 62% increase in EMEA A&P budget to $32m at zero cost to Dell.

  – Enhanced coverage of the brand campaign, delivering greater presence over a longer time period than plan.

  – Designed to enable Dell Germany to benefit from brand launch campaign with minimal P&L impact due to the way funds were scaled, representing saving of over 60% on German media costs in FY00.

➡ Created $13m global sponsorship property at zero cost to Dell (estimated value of worldwide television coverage over race weekend).

  – Dell became Primary Sponsor of 1999 BMW/Williams Le Mans.

  – Created unique customer merchandising opportunities giving away over 2000 Le Mans die cast cars and over 1500 commemorative annuals to key customers.

  – Increased employee morale; most visited EMEA intranet page.

➡ Recognized internally:

"This is the best deal we ever got ... unbeatable ... Let's hurry ... 'Dell was really very dominant as BMW were leading for the total time. Congratulations to a very smart deal.**"**

VP Germany

"I do not think you can get a better deal from any other. We shall go ahead. ... This is great. I look forward to get the revenue from the results.**"**

President, Dell EMEA

Michael demonstrates a bias for action and results and a thirst for winning out the impossible, taking on tough and unfamiliar challenges coupled with seizing opportunities others don't see. Commercial acumen and cultural understanding of the business go hand in hand with a refreshing approach, demonstrating an intellect capable of juggling concepts and complexity. A tenacity to break the mould, to experiment and not accept the status quo is clearly defined. Good quality decisions were made under time pressures and often without full data. There is a creative edge to problem solving, creating a new vision to see and exploit patterns and make associations. This was achieved as he applied 15 years of advertising and marketing knowledge to ground his actions.

There are also a number of start points for separate OAAR analyses. An OAAR could demonstrate the brand equity changes leading to increased brand knowledge and overall value rising within six months. Another OAAR could consider his leadership of the EMEA creative, media and research agencies to plan and execute the campaign resulting in: '. . . delivers well-thought rationale for a planning vision beyond the current quarter . . . working for the greater team goals than personal glory . . . knows European media market . . .'. Another OAAR could demonstrate marketing administration securing over $20m of alliance funding to protocols on budget and to time. Each of these stories would emphasize a set of behaviours that could be drawn upon in different ways from being a good coach of people to strategic ability.

You need to analyze, identify, evaluate and define competencies or groups of competencies. Each OAAR helps you understand your behaviours and base traits and motives. Think back to the type of interview questions you have been asked. There are some classic questions such as 'Have you led a team during a crisis? How did this compare with calmer times?' or 'Tell me about a time you had to deal with conflict.' Think of all the questions that tried to get under your skin and highlight the behaviours you have. Write these questions down. Write down the questions you ask others. Look for the groups of behaviours. Think about how you might respond. Go back to your OAAR analysis. Look for commonly used threads.

Communicates how local issues fit into the bigger picture

Engages and influences the wider community

Ability to negotiate

Provides perspective

Hires best people

Flexibility

Adaptability

Copes with the unexpected

Moves on and is not phased

Intellectual agility

Inclusive and collaborative

Courage

Builds conceptual models

Presents complex concepts in a way that is simple to understand

Ability to deal with ambiguity

Helping others succeed

Resourcefulness

Reduces complexity

Strategic thinker

Works through others to deliver objectives

Commercial awareness

Innovation

Willingness to try different ways when the first way is ineffective

Lateral thinker

Never lets people down

Resources and team management

Inspires team to act; creates common purpose

Results driven

Has a real passion for customers, improving service standards

Never promises what cannot be delivered

Proven ability to lead, coach and develop people

Business builder

Understands people

Loyalty and consistency

Information gathering

Effectively communicates

Ability to promote great team work

Relationship and partnership building

Challenges convention

Ability to influence

Problem solver

Motivating others

Managing and measuring

Decision making

Managing through systems

Planning

Standing alone

Facilitates organizational success

Forward thinking

Identifies viable business opportunities

Juggles complexity

Being comfortable with 80:20 rule

Solves problems not seen before

Stretches team

Cuts to the chase

Understands the questions to ask

Identifies priority actions

Gives others scope and freedom to act

Can discover concepts, trends and patterns

Can draw inferences

Builds relationships

Abstract reasoning

Verbal reasoning

Tenacity to deliver

Tenacity to break the mould

Driven style

Principled

Integrity and trust

Sets priorities

Comfortably handles risk and
uncertainty

Can shift gears

Understands and uses the
informal network to get things
done

It may help if you think how you have been inspired in the past. What makes a great doctor? What made a great boss? Going back in time, you probably respected and responded better to some teachers than others. Which teachers do you still think about and why? Did they involve you? Were the lessons fun? Why were they fun? What did they do to make them fun? Did they pass on a burning passion for their subject and make you want to find out more? Did you gaze at the night sky and dream after a physics lesson at the enormity of the universe?

Step 3 Identify and evidence your Transferable Assets

This last step looks at the frequency with which you have used each competency and at what level of complexity to turn a competency into a Transferable Asset.

A Transferable Asset is a competency you can evidence by demonstrating its use at the same level of complexity across multiple situations. You have a comprehensive OAAR breakdown of your career. You've identified a number of competencies that are evidenced by each OAAR. You can identify a Transferable Asset as a competency you evidence using a number of OAARs taken from a number of companies and roles at the same level of complexity.

Begin by taking
view of

You must begin by taking a helicopter view of your OAARs and look for general patterns and trends. Imagine you are looking down on a field of flowers. Each flower represents the behaviour that you used in your OAAR. Your field will contain many different flowers in a variety of colours. You are looking to group the same coloured flowers together as this demonstrates the competencies you use frequently. The smaller bunches of coloured flowers represent the behaviours that you have demonstrated infrequently. You need to concentrate on the larger bunches of flowers first as these represent the frequency with which you are using the same type of behaviour or group of behaviours and therefore show your strengths.

You'll have a grouping of behaviours that describe a similar way that you did something. Let's assume you have a big bunch of yellow flowers. Each yellow flower is slightly different as it has been picked from a unique OAAR. You now need to distil the competencies down and begin to group the yellow flowers into separate smaller bunches representing a unique competency. Ask yourself: What is the shade of yellow? Are there the same number of petals? What is the tone? You develop and assign revised headings to create and evidence your Transferable Assets.

You will now have identified a Transferable Asset that you have used on several occasions. The complexity of your Transferable Assets is

a helicopter
your OAAR

defined by the type of objectives you regularly deliver. You have a number of OAAR examples that evidence each Transferable Asset. Figure 3.3 illustrates the process. Let's assume you have worked in two

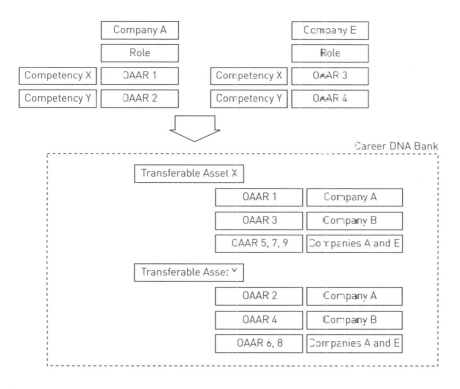

Figure 3.3   Turning competencies into Transferable Assets

companies, A and B. You have created numerous OAAR lists. You have identified two competencies, X and Y, that you are using most. Competency X is evidenced by OAAR 1 from company A and OAAR 3 from company B. Competency Y is evidenced by OAAR 2 from company A and OAAR 4 from company B. Each OAAR is of the same magnitude based on its scope, scale and ambition.

Competency X becomes your Transferable Asset X when you evidence it referencing OAAR 1 and 3 and the further OAARs 5, 7 and 9 from companies A to E.

Competency Y becomes Transferable Asset Y when you evidence it referencing OAAR 2 and 4 and a further two OAAR examples from companies A to E.

Normally you would demonstrate and evidence a Transferable Asset with at least four or five OAAR examples. If you claim to be innovative you will need several OAAR examples at the same level of complexity to evidence this. You will find that you have flashes where you demonstrate a competency at higher level than normal. This does not mean you consistently work at that level. You need to be able to drill down and provide the depth and breadth of your competencies. What would happen if you were asked for another example of this style of competency? And another? And another? Can you demonstrate the same level of complexity in each example?

A number of years ago Michael met with the Chief Operating Officer

Superficiality

of a large international telecommunications company. His Elevator Pitch featured several Transferable Assets and each was in turn evidenced by a couple of short OAAR explanations. In the time available the COO chose to explore one Transferable Asset in detail rather than discuss each at a high level and wanted Michael to talk through not just the OAAR examples he had written about but also to provide further examples of this one Transferable Asset. Whilst this would help him understand the depth of Michael's experience, it also offered a much broader insight into Michael. Michael explained his Transferable Asset using the OAAR technique to structure his answer ensuring the objective was clear, his thinking focused, the action necessary and the result beneficial. Michael amply evidenced his Transferable Asset by talking through four or five clearly structured OAARs.

You need to have some breadth in your Transferable Assets. You need to have some depth of evidence to support your Transferable Assets. Superficiality counts for nothing. Not everyone is results driven. Not everyone is innovative. Not everyone is creative. What are you?

Your Career DNA Bank has been made. It contains 6–10 Transferable Assets and each is evidenced by 4–6 OAAR case studies. Each Transferable Asset is supported with a wealth of information set out in a logical focused manner.

counts for nothing

Your Personal Promise

Your Personal Promise is your executive summary. Like all the best executive summaries it is written last. All Personal Promises are founded on three questions:

➡ Who are you?

➡ How do you do it?

➡ What do you do?

The Personal Promise is like a movie tagline or the opening paragraph of your favourite book. You want to know more. Your Personal Promise is proven by your Transferable Assets, which are in turn evidenced by your OAARs. Your Personal Promise should come from an understanding of your Transferable Assets.

Before we learn how to write your own Personal Promise, let's consider two we have already seen in Chapter 2 and pull them apart.

Bill's Personal Promise is:

"I bring zest for life to my work. I find solutions by understanding which questions need to be asked. 18 years of practical, integrated marketing ideas generation in wide-ranging industry sectors from advertising to publishing throughout the world."

John's Personal Promise is:

"Intelligent risk taker. Direction setter of inventive solutions with the willingness to absorb situations and get on with it. 31 years of leadership of $ multimillion mechanical engineering projects in the international oil industry."

The 'Who are you?' component is answered by 'I bring my zest for life to my work' and 'Intelligent risk taker'. What does this tell you about these two people? One has a sense of fun and passion, and plays hard and works hard, in a larger-than-life outgoing capacity. The second person is more contained in a balanced practical manner and relishes challenges and the associated risk. John is passionate about his customers and what they want, yet he is willing to make that big leap through quantifying the risk.

The second component is 'How do you do it?' This is a summation of your overall competencies at a broad level. Here we have 'I find solutions by understanding which questions need to be asked' and 'Direction setter of inventive solutions with the willingness to absorb situations and get on with it.' What underpins these statements? In order to make things happen, Bill asks general open questions. He asks specific questions. He is curious. He wants to get under the skin of a problem. He is willing to look at things from new perspectives and challenge the way things are done. John's statement shows he is a man who is comfortable and content in fluid situations requiring flexibility of mind balanced by the ability to juggle many balls simultaneously. During all of this he inspires confidence in his team, coupled with the ability to cut to the main issue and assess what is important, why it is important, and how it should be tackled – sometimes in an unorthodox yet highly practical and pragmatic manner.

The third and final question that you need to answer in preparing your Personal Promise is 'What do you do?' It provides the support for the two previous questions. Both have tackled this by showing the length of time, industry sector and geographical regions where they have worked: '18 years of practical, integrated marketing ideas generation for both clients and advertising agencies across the world' and '31 years leadership of $ multimillion mechanical engineering projects in the international oil industry.'

Your Personal Promise should be direct, simple, clear and directional. Your Personal Promise is the conductor and your Transferable Assets are the orchestra. The Personal Promise is your sound bite.

Seems easy enough doesn't it? But let's start in another industry. We've all heard that movies are pitched to studios. Budding writers toil over a story, craft a synopsis and then ruthlessly simplify it down to a core sound bite. The pitch for *Alien* was allegedly 'Jaws in Space'. What does this actually tell us? It had the potential to be a blockbuster, there was sequel potential, it's a thriller based in space with a man-eating monster, a tried and tested storyline, global distribution and the target audience for the film. The fundamental premise is to concentrate on the relationships in your customers' minds and reconnect them in new and exciting ways. Alternatively you could look at how *Alien* was marketed when it was released: 'In space no one can hear you scream' or *Jaws 2* as 'Just when you thought it was safe to go back in the water . . .' What are your few suggestive words? What movie tagline does it for you?

It's excellent practice to play with pitching your favourite movie, book or play in this way so when it comes to you, the whole process is much easier. You'll then find it easier to be ruthlessly selective and only to

The Personal
your

focus on your advantages and benefits. Why not write it down? What did you leave out? And why? What was your focus on? Was it chronological? Autobiographical? Perhaps functional? Did you refer to things you had done and achieved in the past? Or did you focus on how you might be described by your partner? Was it a linear view?

You could have some fun and liken yourself to your favourite superhero; 'Mysteriously flying through task after task, solving problem after problem to keep the company safe at night . . .' which was the start of a Personal Promise for an IT technical support manager, likening his actions to a knight in shining armour correcting the world's rights without the need of praise.

If a tagline can sell a movie, does your Personal Promise sell you? Does your Personal Promise cover the three bases:

→ Who you are

→ How you do it

→ What you do

The first component is 'Who are you?' This is best answered by thinking of examples from other fields and then applying this to yourself. If you were to describe your best friend, how would you describe them? You'd probably focus on a string of adjectives which brought their personality to life rather than their physical description.

Promise is sound bite

If a tagline can
your Personal

It's simple to describe your friends. What would they say about you? Go and grab a book by your favourite author. How have they described their characters and places? There is probably some haunting description you read months ago that lurks in your mind as a powerful evocation of someone's intent. What is yours? How does this translate into your work experience?

To answer the second question 'How do you do it?' you need look at your Transferable Assets. How are you doing things? Are you creating strong morale and spirit in the team? Sharing the successes and learning from the mistakes? Do you create a feeling of belonging? Challenge and stretch people in interesting ways? Lead from the front or the side? Focus on the essential? Make the impossible happen regularly? Think or do? What was the overall pattern of behaviours that you have? Quite simply, how do you do things? What's your fire? Now that you have completed your Transferable Assets you can answer this question.

The third part of the Personal Promise is linear and criteria based. This is a summary of your years of experience, the industry sector or sectors, your profession and perhaps geographical location.

There is no need to have just one Personal Promise. Each Personal Promise you create is tailored for a specific role. Below are a number of

sell a movie, does Promise sell you?

Personal Promises written by people who have made their Elevator Pitches.

"The charm of Bond, the intellect of M, the wit of Q and the looks of Pussy Galore. A sassy cosmopolitan party girl who works hard and plays hard, tackling every challenge and adventure with verve, creativity, persuasion and good humour. Since the age of 10 I have pursued my desire to work as a tabloid journalist.**"**

"I don't make personal promises or claims that I cannot deliver. 13 years as an international investment banker.**"**

"I like to think that dynamic change happens in places I work. I only do jobs I enjoy so I tend to be good at them. I make a difference through strategic guidance which empowers change, through creativity and by motivating my team. I spent 10 years in the Civil Service after gaining my doctorate in law.**"**

"Appetite for mountain-sized challenges being equally fluent in business, finance and technology. 14 years of marketing and management positions in both turnaround and start-up environments, with over 120 clients (corporate, public sector, entrepreneurial and SME).**"**

❝I get the job done. I don't drop the ball. 18 years in the commercial world of fashion and business has given me a wealth of experience. I have a positive outlook and a passion for succeeding.**❞**

❝Creative, down-to-earth leader with sober judgement able to see beneath the surface to create and carry through long-term visions. 11 years in combined operations management, training, HR and market research.**❞**

Career and Education Biography

You need to create a table and populate the following columns:

⇒ Company name

⇒ Dates you worked for them

⇒ Short company description

⇒ Job title

⇒ Job dimensions

⇒ Responsibilities

⇒ Benefit of your job

⇒ Education

Let's consider a couple of these in greater detail.

Short company description

You need a short description of the companies you've worked for. This is for the benefit of the person hiring you, allowing them to construct a summary profile they can forward to others. You are minimizing their workload and helping them with their job. This is especially true if a search firm is involved as they always prepare a written confidential candidate profile for their clients and rarely forward your own CV. You may as well tell the search firm as they have to write it anyway.

The emphasis you give to the one- or two-sentence explanation of the company will depend on the company you are targeting. You could focus on geographic reach, subsidiary of, number of employees, revenue, profit, market share. The statement can be made stronger if you are able to claim the company was, for example, the fastest growing company in EMEA over the last five years, as this confers a quality to you and suggests you played a part in that success.

Job dimensions

You need to include highlights of the key dimensions of your role; who you reported to, their position in the company, the number of direct reports, indirect reports, accountability for budget or P&L; geographical coverage, multi-unit, multi-channel, multi-site, international . . .

Responsibilities and benefits

You should list all of your responsibilities and perhaps group some of your responsibilities into categories such as business process outsourcing, supplier negotiation and procurement or business transformation.

Next you should write a statement that expresses these responsibilities as a benefit to the organization, showing how your responsibilities manifest themselves for the organization. What was the benefit of employing you? This is not the same as the results you delivered. Results are more detailed orientated and you need to 'chunk up' your results to gain the business benefit. The best way to think of this is to

What was the employing

imagine asking your boss what they think you are doing. They would rarely express this as a feature and would be more interested in the benefit.

What else do you need to know?

There are a number of other considerations you need to address and think through.

Visual Impact

Create a layout and appearance that is designed to be read. Use a clear and legible common typeface at a reasonable size such as Arial 11 pt. Leave sensible margins. Ensure your words have the 'air' to breathe. Don't cramp your words as you strike a balance between space and text. Clearly separate out different elements of your story. Use a consistent structure throughout for headings and bullets. Don't use shading or boxes. Think of someone speed reading for 15 to 30 seconds. Do you have their attention? Have you designed it to be read? What is their eye drawn to? Is that phrase the one you'd like someone who didn't know you to read first? What will they remember about you 10 minutes from now? What would you like them to remember 10 minutes from now?

benefit of you?

You should check what your Elevator Pitch CV looks like when converted to plain text and you should check the tabulations, avoid tables, avoid reversing the text to make it white type out of a black box and use italics sparingly.

Words. Personality. Tone

Create simple short sentences that are well written. Create simple short sentences that sound great. Create a good story told well. Every word matters. There is power in what you do not say. Use bullet points to abbreviate and condense. Use action words rather than passive words. Include keywords where needed. Do not add anything that will give a reason for you to be excluded. Do not omit anything, such as unexplained periods, that will give a reason for you to be excluded. You are making a compelling story where each element is crafted in its own right and all elements, when taken together, add up to being greater than the sum of the parts. Ensure you focus on what will grab their attention, highlighting your priority points. Don't swamp people in detail.

Look around and ask why so many companies sound dry and bland through the abstracted, colourless and lifeless words that fail to communicate. Where is the passion? Where is the intensity and directness? Where does a company find its intonation? Where does a company find its posture? People often strip away their personality and pull on a bland white mask when thinking about themselves in a work context. Emotions are not allowed. Passion is missing. Why wear a cloak of invisibility? What makes you want to become colourless? Make sure you inject a vodka shot of personality into your Elevator Pitch. If your Elevator Pitch is devoid of your personality and chemistry, why don't you send someone else, with a similar skill profile, to do your interview? You'd like the person hiring you to be able to see, hear, taste or feel you working in their team when they open your cover letter or read your CV. Wouldn't you rather work for someone who liked how you came across? Isn't recruitment a two-way street? On certain occasions Michael has used phrases such as 'Fiscal magic acclaimed internally . . .' when describing one of the outcomes of his work at Dell. He knew this would become a focal point to explain and expand one of his Transferable Assets.

You need to be prudent. We are not advocating snazzy adjectives peppering an application as this is just filler. As an exercise you should delete any adjective you have used and see if the sentence is improved. Say each sentence out aloud. Practise what you might say in front of a mirror. Eliminate words that embellish and fill. Examine each sentence and each word. Combine sentences together and condense and shorten them. Be judicious and ruthless in which words you will include and

Inject a vodka shot into your

what you will exclude. Use words to create pictures. Ask 'So what?' or 'Well, you would say that wouldn't you!' all the time. If it does not feel right, drop the word or rewrite the sentence.

Make your words come alive. You will see in the next chapter that you will create much of the information you can use to answer an interview question. You need to rehearse and make it all feel natural. Sit in front of a mirror and speak out loudly. Sleep on your words. Write them in another way. Ensure you have enough time to make your presentation as good as the content. Never be satisfied with your words; they can nearly always be improved.

Finally, would you write the word 'letter' at the top of a letter? Precisely. You shouldn't think that CVs somehow break the norm.

Length

Brevity counts. A 1 to 2 page Elevator Pitch. A 30 to 60 second answer to 'What do you do?' A 2 to 3 minute response to the interview question 'Tell me about yourself.' A 3 to 4 paragraph cover letter.

Facts

Stick to your facts.

# of personality
Elevator Pitch

Family and interests

You should include these if they are relevant or you have an interesting or unusual hobby. Sometimes being in your early 40s and married with kids demonstrates a stability the company is looking for and a belief you have at least another two big roles within you. Include date of birth if you wish. Be aware of the legislation and the norms in your country and what is or is not required.

Contact details

If there is ambiguity over your first name and it is not possible to tell whether you are male or female, you should include your title. Again you need to be respectful of the legislation in your country. Normally contact details are on the first page at the top and should include address, contact numbers and e-mail addresses.

Photographs

In some continental European countries a photograph is normally required. In many other countries it is not accepted practice.

You are competing unique

Education and publications

List courses, key establishments and grades. Don't list every training course you have attended unless they are relevant to the position you are aiming for. Once you have work experience, school exams matter little. Use your judgement.

Critique your building blocks

You have created and developed a consistent foundation to help you at any stage of the recruitment process. You have created a set of building blocks that you can assemble in any way to communicate to your next employer that you have the competencies, skills, knowledge, experience, ability and personality for the job and for their company. Good communication is about what you say, when you say it, to whom you say it, and how you say it. You are competing to find your unique turf, the spot that is not already occupied by someone else. You are about to make their buying decision easier and more satisfying. You help your buyer perceive you as superior through helping them achieve clarity.

You have created your Personal Promise. Your Transferable Assets are sitting in your Career DNA Bank. You have a Career Biography.

to find your turf

You now have a set of great building blocks to help you create unique and tailored Elevator Pitches for each step of the recruitment process. In the next chapter you'll see how you can bundle them up to create your Elevator Pitch.

chapter

Targeting your Elevator Pitch

You will learn

➡ How to assemble your Elevator Pitch

➡ How to target and tailor your Elevator Pitch

How to assemble your Elevator Pitch

Fitting it together

To create your Elevator Pitch you need to build the foundations. Any strong building is built on strong foundations. Figure 4.1 shows you how all the building blocks fit together.

On the right-hand side of Figure 4.1 are your building blocks. These are the specific building blocks of your Elevator Pitch that you will use at each and every step of the recruitment process.

➡ Your Personal Promise based on the three core components of who you are, how you do it and what you have done

➡ Your Transferable Assets, based on competencies you can evidence which are stored in your Career DNA Bank

➡ Your Career Biography containing key work details

On the left-hand side of Figure 4.1 is the company you are hoping to work for. You might be responding to an advertisement or contacting them speculatively. From your research, and perhaps reading an advertisement, you will know some interesting information. You will know:

➡ Their Corporate Promise based on the three components of who they are, what they do and how they do it

➡ Their Job DNA described by the business and technical competencies which are in turn partly based on the knowledge, skills, abilities and personality they need in order to deliver their

Your Elevator Pitch

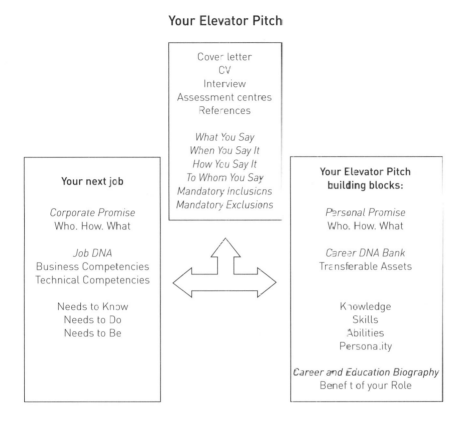

Cover letter
CV
Interview
Assessment centres
References

What You Say
When You Say It
How You Say It
To Whom You Say
Mandatory Inclusions
Mandatory Exclusions

Your next job

Corporate Promise
Who. How. What

Job DNA
Business Competencies
Technical Competencies

Needs to Know
Needs to Do
Needs to Be

**Your Elevator Pitch
building blocks:**

Personal Promise
Who. How. What

Career DNA Bank
Transferable Assets

Knowledge
Skills
Abilities
Personality

Career and Education Biography
Benefit of your Role

Figure 4.1 Answering 'What do you offer me?'

Corporate Promise. This is often summarized in a job description based on what you need to know, need to do and need to be

You will see there is a high degree of similarity between these two columns. To get the job you want, you need to bridge the gap between these two columns with your Elevator Pitch. They want you to answer 'What do you offer me?' You need to get into your next employer's shoes. You know you need to speak their language, write your words, mirror their actions and meet their needs. You need to help them at each and every step of the recruitment process. You know they want to know how you will help them based on evidence of your past behaviours and results.

You need to speak

You prove to them you have what they want. You evidence you have what they want by focusing on your true differentiating qualities. You innovatively bundle your Transferable Assets to make your next employer buy you. You answer 'What do you offer me?' You show

➡ You are their 'how'

➡ You are their 'who'

➡ You have the 'what'

➡ You have been at the 'where'

Personal Details

Personal Promise
What do you offer them?

Transferable Assets
Transferable Asset 1 (2 examples to demonstrate and evidence)
Transferable Asset 2 (2 examples to demonstrate and evidence)
Transferable Asset 3 (2 examples to demonstrate and evidence)
Transferable Asset 4 (2 examples to demonstrate and evidence)

Chronological Career

Education

Hobbies

Figure 4.2   The core elements of your Elevator Pitch CV

their language

You need to create a bespoke Elevator Pitch for every company and position you apply for. However, it's useful to create a generic Elevator Pitch CV as shown in Figure 4.2 by imagining you are applying for the type of job you'd like to have at the company you'd like to work for.

Choose the best Transferable Assets and the best OAAR examples that prove them from your Career DNA Bank. By now each OAAR has been written using active language, written in the third person, and crafted several times. The story it tells is short, focused and specific. For your Elevator Pitch CV you need to make it even sharper and shorter and pivot it through 180 degrees. You turn your OAAR to lead on the result, so it becomes RAAO. You lead on the result and then explain how you delivered the result. It is your discretion on how much or how little and which part of the AAO you include. Figure 4.3 shows your Career DNA Bank, the Transferable Assets you have chosen and the reverse OAARs.

For example, you could have as a RAAO: 'Decreased headcount 10% year on year following rigorous department audit'. In the last chapter you saw an OAAR analysis regarding Bill and Fairfax. If we apply the same principle, this is how they might look as a statement on an Elevator Pitch. Bill took the OAAR analysis and used that to create the first example of his Transferable Assets:

Your Elevator Pitch CV/Application Form
Condensed OAAR turned 180 degrees

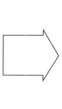

Identified Transferable Assets for New Job

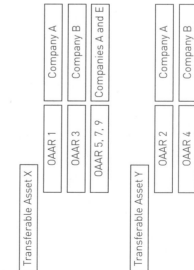

Figure 4.3 Using your Career DNA Bank

Concise message delivery

"Won new business of Fairfax, Australia's leading Newspaper group when they approached Bates Advertising Agency. Devised strategy to provide a seamless flow of information, regardless of location or time zone, enabling Fairfax to sell more media space more effectively than before."

Encapsulate everything in your Personal Promise. You may also want to create a second generic Elevator Pitch as there are times when your career could move in several directions.

Your generic Elevator Pitch is not sent to anyone and is solely created to give you a great template.

Your Elevator Pitch should have a resonance which you feel. If you gave it to your friends, without your name on the top, would they be able to identify you? Your Elevator Pitch is like a mirror and if your reflection is cloudy you should rethink your words and actions. You will know when it feels right and your colleagues and friends could easily confirm this.

The recruitment process is not about your generic Elevator Pitch as competencies are specific to your new role and you need to tailor what your next employer is looking for with what you have. To bridge the gap in Figure 4.1 you must do your research.

Research

You can find virtually anything on any company from their corporate web sites, search engines, and databases. Study the company. Look at their competitors. Get a feel for the industry. Understand their strategy. Read the annual reports. Listen to their web casts, paying attention to the analyst Q&A sessions as they are often a rich source of

Study the
Look at their

information on key issues and concerns. Read the biographies of the executive team and anyone who could interview you. Use your network to find out what you can about the company. Do you know people who work for them? If so, give them a call and take them out for a drink.

You may have a job ad in front of you. Analyze it carefully and see what the accountabilities are, what skills they need, experiences they want and what competencies they are looking for.

Find out as much as you can from as many sources as you can and create a dossier on the company and make sure you cover the following two areas.

Corporate Promise

Who. How. What.

Job DNA

➡ Business competencies

➡ Technical competencies

➡ What you need to know, to do and to be

➡ Highlight specific phrases or words that they use

➡ Make sure your dossier is a list of everything the company wants you to demonstrate

company.
competitors

How to target and tailor your Elevator Pitch

You can now begin to adapt and tailor your Elevator Pitch for each company ensuring each step you take is correct.

Elevator Pitch

It is best to create your Elevator Pitch CV before you write your cover letter. The role of your Elevator Pitch CV is to get an interview. Your Elevator Pitch CV evidences how you meet the job requirements by relating your past achievements and how you achieved these results to the role. Your benefit is in how you meet and exceed the role specification.

The first step is to take the list of everything you have discovered about the company and match these with your Transferable Assets. Look at everything in your Career DNA Bank. You need to match their Job DNA with your Career DNA. What Transferable Assets are the best ones for the role? Do you have the proof that they need? Do you have the breadth of Transferable Assets? Do you have the depth they want?

The second step is to look at the words the company uses to describe its Job DNA. You want your Transferable Assets and any details from your Career Biography to reflect the language the company has used. Add to your Transferable Assets any words or phrases that the company uses in their Job DNA. It is a process of constantly rewriting and juggling how you describe your Transferable Assets to tailor them to your next employer. You should check any keywords the company has used to describe the role and amend any of the words in your career details.

The third step is to create your Personal Promise. Your Personal Promise is evidenced by your Transferable Assets. Your Personal Promise is also matched against their Corporate Promise.

You now have a tailored Elevator Pitch. The content is spot on. The structure is clear. Everything you are telling your next employer is evidenced. All the evidence is substantiated. It is written from the perspective of your next employer in a language they understand. You clearly answer their question 'What do you offer me?'

Cover letter

Your cover letter's only job is to get your Elevator Pitch read. Your cover letter tells your next employer 'I can do this based on this in my past'. It tells them how you meet their corporate requirements by relating your experience directly to the need of the organization.

Your letter is always written to a named person. You know their names and titles as you've done your research.

Your cover letter's get your Elevator

A cover letter clearly signposts and highlights specific parts of your Elevator Pitch making short, sharp and incisive connections back to their needs. Your cover letter gives a brief overview of your understanding of the company and the role and states clearly why you are applying. You must inspire and grab their attention in 3–4 paragraphs.

A strong opening paragraph matches their Corporate Promise with your Personal Promise by turning your Personal Promise into a benefit for them. If someone has referred you to the company, mention them by name.

In the second paragraph make sure you explicitly refer to any particular skills, knowledge, experience or competencies they are looking for. Tick them off on the list you made. Tell them you have what they want.

In the third paragraph express your interest in helping the company do more and the part you'd play in their ongoing success. Convey to them you want to work for them not just anyone in their industry.

You need to round it off with a call to action that is polite and firm but not pushy.

Application form

Completing an application form follows the same process as your Elevator Pitch.

**only job is to
Pitch read**

Go through the application form noting down all the information they want. Extract the best Transferable Assets from your Career DNA Bank that explain each point. You may need to rephrase or rewrite them. Look carefully at each sentence you have used to support each Transferable Assets and assess which are best utilized to make each point and at which point on the application form. From your Career Biography extract the key dates and places you were employed.

If you are completing an application form online, you should create a Word document with all the relevant information taken from your Career DNA Bank. Then copy and paste the right sections.

A University Careers Manager was recently completing an application form and asked for our advice. We advised them to create their Career DNA Bank. The application form was easily completed as the evidence required to support each point was clearly organized in their Career DNA Bank. There was a clear match between the person's Personal Promise and Transferable Assets and the Corporate Promise and Job DNA. Our friend was shortlisted instantly and secured the new position.

Interviews

Your interview proves how you meet the job requirements by relating your past achievements and how you achieved these results to the role

There is no a typical

and to the person you meet. There is no such thing as a typical interview. You could meet the search firm, the client, be interviewed by one person or by a panel. You could be asked many questions across several topics.

Undoubtedly you will be asked about your experience and you will explore your work history. Your career biography contains the benefit of your role to your last company as well as the list of your responsibilities. It is better to talk about benefits as this demonstrates the importance of your role to the organization and the part you played in ensuring the company was successful.

You will be asked to describe past work situations and explain your behaviours. Sometimes the questions might be hypothetical and ask you to describe your probable response to a situation. You may be asked what you learnt from your experience.

There are several ways your Career DNA Bank helps you during the interview. Your Elevator Pitch CV can be expanded into a crib sheet for your interview by taking the full OAAR analyses directly from your Career DNA Bank. This enables you to recall the key points you'd like to put across and provides a library of great answers to their questions.

You might be subject to a Case Study interview. You will be told of a situation. Information is likely to be missing. You need to listen, clarify, think, hypothesize, analyze, probe, evaluate, frame, communicate,

such thing as interview

challenge, look at the issue from their perspective, form intelligent opinions and present recommendations. Your Career DNA Bank proves invaluable as you already know your strongest areas. However, the most important lesson for successfully dealing with a case study is to examine the issue from the shoes of the person whose problem you are solving. You've just done this when you created your new Elevator Pitch. You thought like the person who was about to offer you a job and tried to understand their perspective to find the right solution.

The *Guardian* newspaper in the UK wrote:

"It certainly paid off for 29-year-old Louise Medley. A sales professional in a male-dominated sector, she wanted to break into a new market, but lacked confidence about her ability. So she sat down and wrote out her own elevator pitch. 'Once you've written it, in a sense the job of selling yourself is done . . . it really brought home to me how many things I can do.' Shortly after producing her elevator pitch, Medley landed a new job. 'They did seem to be pretty impressed – I was more or less offered the job straightaway,' she says. 'Of course, I don't know if I would have got the job using a CV – but I wouldn't have gone into the interview with such confidence if I hadn't done the preparation in producing my elevator pitch.'"

Your Career DNA
you with all

Assessment centres

Assessment centres are used to compile a comprehensive picture in relation to your job performance and potential, drawn from a range of sources and tests. These sources include behavioural interviewing, case study interviewing, work simulation, psychometric profiling, personality tests, ability tests, interest inventories to the social inter-action over lunch, coffee and dinner.

Ability tests measure current ability and future potential for different types of work skills such as verbal reasoning or spatial awareness. Interest inventories assess your likes and dislikes of certain work activities. Personality tests profile your perception of your behaviour and style within a workplace. Psychometric tests measure mental abilities, personality traits, motives and interests. Sometimes some of these tests might be administered independently of any assessment centre. Whilst your Career DNA Bank will not directly help you prepare for the above tests, it will help you understand the feedback so you should not have any surprises.

Your Career DNA Bank provides you with all your ammunition to successfully answer any behavioural interviewing questions. Take your Career DNA Bank with you to the assessment centre and refresh your memory of your strengths the evening before. Also remember to take

Bank provides your ammunition

along your company research dossier and remind yourself of their needs and concerns. You'll probably spot the competency sets they are looking for in each exercise. An MBA student from Imperial College London applied for an Analyst position at BT and attended an Assessment Day. She could see which competencies were being tested. She could clearly express her own Transferable Assets as she had prepared her Career DNA Bank. She had a clear understanding of her strengths. She excelled, progressed to the final interview stage, and was offered the position.

"It's more than writing a CV. It's about being able to understand yourself, writing my Career DNA bank enabled me to think more systematically about my experiences and be successful in the assessment day and interview."

Mahsa Gharebaghi, Imperial College London

References

The role of your referee is to confirm that they observed and acknowledged that what you said is true.

You should use your bespoke Elevator Pitch to brief your referees. You should send it to them with a note on the company you are applying for. You should explain what the company is trying to achieve and looking for. You should tell them why you match the company's profile. You should help your referees by making all the connections and links for them. You also need to think which referee it is best to use to confirm which bit of your story. You'll want to customize your briefing documents to each referee.

They are busy people. You'd like your referees to spend their time talking about you not analyzing you. Make it easy for them. You've done the hard work. You understand yourself. You've researched the company. You've made the links. Tell your referees.

When the referee is called for a reference they will have clear relevant and targeted information that supports everything you have told your next employer.

chapter

5

Top-floor Elevator Pitches

We would like to welcome all of you who thought this was the first page of the book. We know this is an easy mistake that any one of us could make. We would recommend a look at the rest of the book, as it is really quite helpful.

In this second edition we have taken our concepts and ideas further than the first edition as we have learned more about this evolving market and this is reflected in the choice of the Elevator Pitches. Each one has been designed to be a hard-hitting, no-fuss, no-nonsense strategic personal sales document applicable to that person. We would like to thank all our friends and colleagues for all their help in this chapter. Each one is different as it is an approach that is designed to be flexible rather than rigidly applied.

The Elevator Pitches are from real people from many walks of life across the globe. They range from pilots to office managers, from entre-preneurs to advertising people, from mechanical engineers to veterinary nurses, from publishers to politicians, from management consultants to business analysts. They demonstrate the flexibility and universal approach of the Elevator Pitch and the people who use it.

Neil Howlin*:	Management Consultant, Capgemini
Darren Fell:	Founder of Pure360.com (digital marketing)
David Shairp*:	Global Strategist: J P Morgan Asset Management
Justine Cobb*:	Admin Manager
Fiona Murie*:	Management Consultant
Michael Matthews*:	Graduate in a leading Investment Management Company
Bill Faust:	Marketing Consultant and Guest Speaker

Ana Molina*:   Cabin Crew

John Baldwin*:   Senior Mechanical Engineer, Vetco

Albertus Zwiers*:   Fleet Manager Supply Ships Maersk

Ken Livingstone: Mayor of London

Marc Schavemaker: Commercial Airline Pilot (747) for British
                    Airways

Louise Medley*:   Sales, Vent-Axia

Laura Neilson*:   Veterinary Nurse and Pet Insurance Sales
                    Representative

Christine Coleman*: Manager, Luxury Retail

Most of the following Elevator Pitches can be printed on one or two sides of paper. *All these people have used the Elevator Pitches featured in the following pages to help them get their current position.

NEIL HOWLIN

The Cottage, 99 Boxtown Road, London E24 3DA

+44 (0) 7775 XXXXX, neil_howlin@temachin.com

Appetite for mountain-sized challenges being equally fluent in business, finance and technology. Fourteen years of marketing and management positions in both turnaround and start-up environments, with over 120 clients (corporate, public sector, entrepreneurial and SME).

Results-focused (from sales to process improvement)

- Achieved personal objective of graduating at top of full-time MBA class (jointly with team-mate) at Henley Management College by combining commitment and discipline with analytical insight. (2003–2004)

- Exceeded profit targets for three consecutive years by up to 225% at Metrocube, an internet incubator, by understanding each client's business needs (explicit and latent) and creating profitable services to fulfil them. (2000–2003)

Transforming strategic analysis into creative solutions

- Increased estimated IPO valuation of Loewy Group (marketing services) by up to £1m (10%) by challenging their acquisition integration strategy, supporting the case by identifying key valuation metrics from market peers. Developed an implementation plan to maximize market perception of value – now adopted. (2004–2005)

- Won business from Sun Microsystems, Honeywell, Kenwood and Unisys after launching a new media agency 'IO', a subsidiary of Ideal Solutions. Created an innovative e-marketing service making IO client websites sales focused. (1998–2000)

Building client relationships (up to PLC board level)

- Developed over 40 long-term client relationships at Ideal Solutions, generating up to £1m annual fee income and building credibility by demonstrating extensive understanding of clients' business issues, technologies and customer needs. (1994–2000)

- Repeatedly re-hired by former employers/clients as freelance consultant. (2003-present)

Creating committed teams in high-pressure environments

- Increased sense of ownership and trust at Metrocube, reversed a declining profit trend, enabled business to outperform market during the economic downturn in 2001. Coached team and transformed flagging morale into motivated, self-reliant individuals by engaging them in the business process development.

- 5,100 people signed up to the Project 'BeyondBricks.com' supported by £1.5m DTI funding to stimulate internet entrepreneurship. Led web-portal development and operations team formed from consortium members. Developed UK-wide partnership network for content and event sponsorship to extend reach of budget (2001–2003)

Financial Acumen and Awareness

- Focused on finance during MBA to add formal knowledge to hands-on experience. Leveraged experience of managing £2m P&L and projects up to £1.5m to understand corporate finance issues at enterprise scale. Gained maximum grades for both business finance elective module and for dissertation researching acquisition valuation. (2004)

- Directed £0.5m expansion project at Metrocube, established second incubation centre financed only from cash flow. Overcame crisis situation caused by profound setbacks, complicated by the need to fulfil a client commitment. Motivated team of direct and third-party staff to exceptional performance and long hours. Continual situational awareness, aggressive budget management and negotiation with suppliers ensured client commitments were kept whilst company remained cash flow positive throughout. (2001)

Career History

Project experience includes merger integration, new business launches, strategic analysis, brand repositioning, infra-structure design, marketing and CRM programmes, business restructuring, process development and re-engineering.

Sector experience includes IT (hardware, software and services), public sector, marketing services, distribution channels, e-commerce, new media and consumer products.

Capgemini: Senior Consultant   Sep 2005 – present

Third largest management and technology consultancy. Joined Transformation Consulting team.

Consulting projects   Mar 2003 – Aug 2005

Clients include Loewy Group (advertising), T-Mobile, Servo Group (IT services) and Carrenza (technology consultancy). Hired by the Henley Centre for Business to conduct commissioned research on Information Assurance for Qinetiq and Business Continuity Management for AXA.

Full-time MBA, Henley Management College   Jul 2003 – Jan 2005

One of Europe's top business schools and one of the world's most international MBAs, including study in South Africa, USA, Australia and China. Graduated joint first in class and member of top-performing team.

COO & CTO, Metrocube   Apr 2000 – Mar 2003

Business incubator for internet start-ups. Joined management team at launch and steered £2m P&L through consistent positive cash flow generation until exit in 2003 through trade sale. Led direct team of 8 and up to 30 indirect/third party reports.

Account Director, Ideal Solutions   **Jan 1993 – Mar 2000**

Integrated marketing and advertising agency – joined as first employee. Managed 150+ marketing and CRM projects for blue-chip IT sector clients including Oracle, Granada plc, Compel plc, Honeywell, SCO, MDIS and Lotus/IBM. Recruited and developed account teams to grow business to 20 employees and £1.5m revenue.

Education

Master of Business Administration, Henley Management College (2005)
Business courses in Sales, Presentation and Negotiation (1996–1998)

Outside work

Ten years as member of charitable theatre group supporting local causes. Passionate snowboarder.

Darren Fell

Pure, Dolphin House, 2–5 Manchester Street, Brighton BN2 1TF

Tel: 0870 765 7222, E-mail: darren.fell@pure360.com

I am an ideas generator capable of turning dreams into reality. I inspire others through excitement and enthusiasm to create highly skilled teams. I am determined and never give up and my forte is delivering outstanding results. Twelve years in high-profile business development and entrepreneurial roles, founder and now Sales and Marketing Director of Pure.

Company builder – start from scratch and grow

- Successfully demonstrated the need for email and text marketing. In 2000 realized my ambition and founded my own business. To test initial idea, set up a pilot company and built a prototype that allowed party organizers to manage party invites and to distribute reminders and promotions via email and text messages.

- In 2001 Pure360.com was born. A business plan mapping the company's future growth was written and investment won. The initial development team and system specification were put together, the email and SMS system was created and Pure won its first blue chip-clients.

Self belief – I will invest everything I've got

- My belief in the viability of Pure was so great that for the first year I financed the whole project by using all of my savings and re-mortgaging my home.

- To achieve and exceed expectations, I worked 70-hour weeks for 18 months to create a strong foundation for the business.

Always employ smarter people

- To enable high-volume email and SMS deliveries and take on a large customer base, it was imperative to employ a Technical Director to build a scalable system. An exceptionally talented Architect and Developer was appointed and further key technical team members hired. This allowed Pure360.com to considerably increase its revenue stream. (2003)

- To take Pure's expansion to the next level and keep ahead of its competitors in terms of product evolution, a highly experienced Managing Director was brought in to safely manage the growth of the business in all aspects. This enabled the original team members to focus on their key areas and Pure to expand. (2005)

Uncovering opportunities

- I moved to the position of Sales Director and this simple move increased sales by 400%. To maximize our true potential, prior to an outside MD being appointed, I questioned the resource allocation to ensure the team were working to their strengths at all times. My strengths lay in selling, whilst most of my time had been involved managing the company. The Technical Director, also a trained accountant, was made Managing Director to oversee the running of the company. (2004)

- Raised company awareness and won major new clients such as RS Components, who use Pure's system in 32 countries. To make Pure known to its customer base, with limited funds studied UK sponsorship opportunities. Signed deals with The Edinburgh International Film Festival, Brighton Festival and Fringe and cult gossip web site Popbitch. This gave them free or subsidized use of the email and mobile marketing system in return for Pure's branding on every message sent.

Career History

Pure (pure360.com) 2000 – present (including proof of concept)
Founder and Sales & Marketing Director

Colt Telecom 2000 – 2001
European Account Manager

GX Networks 1999 – 2000
Account Manager

Bates Australia 1998 – 1999
E Commorce Director

Morse Computers 1996 – 1998
Account Manager

Frontier Internet Services 1995–1996 (Shareholder, company recently sold to Mistral Internet)
Sales Manager

Cable & Wireless (Mercury Communications) 1989 – 1995
Maintenance Engineer to Sales Engineer

DAVID SHAIRP

20 years' investment experience as a fund manager, economist, strategist and research director gleaned literally from the four corners of the world. Strong track record in leading teams and increasing companies' profitability, distinguished by strong analytical and communication skills and enhanced by the world-class Sloan Fellowship programme at London Business School.

Expertise in investment processes

- Advised on a mandate to invest $60m by selecting three funds of hedge fund for a major European bank, using a proprietary methodology.

- Developed and published an acclaimed Sloan Master's research thesis on UK fund management performance, working with Mercer Investment Consulting and top investors, to assess the effect of personality and investment process on performance.

- Created and implemented new EMEA and European strategy processes, with proprietary new currency and market sentiment indicators.

- Re-engineered Asian economic framework to fit into an emerging markets fixed-income product. Developed client relationships that helped lead to a doubling in BZW's commission income and firm profit.

Analytical and independent thinking

- Won the Accenture award for the best Sloan strategic management report.

- Advised the Malaysian government on how to solve its balance of payments crisis at the height of the Asian crisis. Proposals were adopted in full in the fiscal package.

- Pioneered a regional Asian equity strategy publication, using an original framework. Rated as No 1 economist/strategist in Asia by global fund managers and held consistently high ratings over a 5-year period.

Team leadership

◆ Increased productivity and reduced employee turnover, with 12 years' experience creating and developing high performance teams, ranging from 4 to 60+ people.

◆ Managed and worked with colleagues of over 35 nationalities.

◆ Coordinated successful launch preparations of EMEA business as deputy to the boss who was temporarily on leave. Managed EMEA research team with a consequent 25% increase in productivity within 3 months.

◆ Devised a robust business plan for BZW's Asian research to improve productivity and client penetration. Achieved top-5 ranking and raised market share.

Communication skills

◆ Delivered acclaimed presentations at international conferences, including the CBI, GSIC, BZW global strategy conference.

◆ Appeared frequently on TV and in the print media, including CNN, CNBC, the *Financial Times*, and *South China Morning Post*.

◆ Presented regularly to institutional clients in 43 international financial centres.

Personal details: Born: 4 November 1959. Married with three children

Contact details: Tree Grange, Woods Lane, East Sussex

Tel: 44 (0) xxx xxx xx Mobile: 44 (0) xxx xxx
Email: DShairp.sln2003@london.edu

Education: London Business School, Sloan Masters (MSc) Programme in Management; Exeter University, BA (Hons) Economics (2:1); London Stock Exchange examinations

Career details

Consultant   Financial Services   2003 – 2004

- Carried out detailed due diligence for a major European bank on a €210m fund of hedge funds, prior to creating a CPPI structured product.

- Developed a proprietary methodology for FoHF selection and helped a major bank select three FoHFs for an initial investment of $60m.

- Conducted series of psychometric personality tests for Investec's UK Equity team and presented the findings and implications at business strategy offsite.

- Devised a business plan for a leading UK private bank, to transform its business from being banking-led to investment-led.

London Business School   Sloan Fellow London   2002 – 2003

- Won Accenture team award for the best Sloan strategic management report.

- Published an acclaimed research thesis on UK fund management performance, to assess the effect of personality and investment process on performance.

- Consulted for a leading clothing brand and developed its e-commerce strategy.

BNP Paribas   Strategist, Chief Economist & Head of Research London and Hong Kong   1998 – 2002

- Led 10-person EMEA research team, oversaw 25% increase in productivity.

- Led a 13-person cross-functional team to create an extensive research publication on Austria's market and top stocks for a successful Paris conference.

- Implemented a new European strategy publication, which gained client recognition and led to account openings.
- Led a four-man economics team, based in London and Hong Kong, tripling research productivity in 1999 and pioneering an original new electronic publication, while firm was in process of being acquired.

Caspian Securities Ltd   **Partner and Asia Strategist**   **1997 – 1998**
Singapore and London

- Invited to become a partner in the world's first global internet investment bank.
- Acted as an Economic Adviser to the Malaysian government prior to its December 1997 fiscal package. Recommendations were adopted in full.

BZW Asia Limited   **Regional Research Director/Asia Strategist**   **1990 – 1996**
Hong Kong and Singapore

- Improved overall research penetration, with top-5 rankings and gained market share. Successfully led 10 corporate research teams (60 analysts) from 1991/94.
- Pioneered a regional equity strategy product using an original framework approach and was voted the top economist/strategist in Asia in 1992/93.

UBS-Phillips & Drew   **Far East Economist**   **1984 – 1990**
London and Hong Kong

- Member of the no. 1-rated team. Created Asian economic product from scratch, which was well regarded by institutions and governments.

James Capel & Co   **Private Client & Pension Fund Manager**   **1982 – 1984**
London

JUSTINE COBB

66 The Look Out, Birling Gap, Sussex, UK

Telephone: 01321xxx xxx

Email: justine.cobb@virgin.net

I get the job done. I don't drop the ball. Eighteen years in the commercial world of fashion and business has given me a wealth of experience. I have a positive outlook and a passion for succeeding.

Effective communications: written and verbal

- Ensured new recruits were fully briefed and became effective team members. Created, wrote and presented the office induction material incorporating company policy, procedures, health and safety, departmental responsibilities etc. (Infoline, 1999–2005)

- Gained 'Investors in People' accreditation in 2004 leading the successful deployment and implementation within Infoline. Lead contact with the assessor, set up funding through Sussex Enterprise and gained company buy-in through presentations and written documents.

Organizational agility: working to deadlines; initiative as occasion demands

- Organized and oversaw the coordination of between 90 and 120 event days a year. Involved scheduling and overseeing all activities. Event dates were fixed so it was imperative to hit deadlines, manage risk and stick to strict budgets. This was a daily necessity of my role. (Infoline, 1999–2005)

- Project managed refurbishment and move to a new office for Infoline Conferences. Coordinated transfer of telephone numbers, broadband connection, IT network, staff and furniture. Had to ensure people knew what to do and when to do it, as well as managed activities of third-party suppliers.

Problem-solving skills: taking an optimistic and realistic approach

- To improve accuracy, save time and develop the team's IT knowledge, introduced a Macro in a spreadsheet. Once team knew how to create a macro, they were looking for any opportunity to use one.

- Arranged transport for staff and delegates caught up in the terrorist attacks of 7 July 2005 in London. 250 delegates and 6 members of staff needed to get home from central London. Ensured delegates had access to key emergency service information and made sure staff members could give information to their colleagues and families via our office in Eastbourne. Juggled existing arrangements to get delegates out of the city to stations and airports then safely home.

Good financial numeracy

- Assisted the Managing Director of Infoline in setting the budget and controlling spend of an £80,000 office refurbishment.

- Initially processed all sales invoices and payment receipts for the conferences. As company grew, recruited and managed the new financial controller who provided all the accounts for the company.

- Worked to tight budgetary controls: for venue hire, negotiated fees for suppliers and promotion spend. Monitored all outgoings and incomings and broke down all the figures into easily measurable units; cost per paying delegate.

Career Summary

Infoline Conferences Ltd   **October 1999 to August 2005**

Operations Manager

Accountable to the Managing Director, I had overall responsibility for the running of the Operations Department.

Management of a team covering all aspects relating to the logistical and technical co-ordination of each of the company's events.

Office and building management.

Human Resources – recruitment, health and safety, fire procedures.

Customer excellence initiatives, Investors in People, business recovery planning.

Claremont Garments   March 1990 to March 1999
(Major lingerie and children's wear supplier to Marks & Spencer Plc)

Technical/Quality Assurance Manager (May 1995 – 1999)
Responsible for the implementation and production of new styles, from both a quality and technical aspect for two factories.
Technical Manager (October 1997 – August 1998)
Account Manager (September 1994 – April 1995)
Grading Manager (March 1990 – August 1994)

Jaeger Tailoring Limited   September 1987 to February 1990

Unbranded Designer/Pattern Cutter
Creating classic Jaeger-style dresses and suit collections for Mark & Spencer Plc.

Education

London College of Fashion: B/TEC HND Clothing Technology
                              B/TEC OND Clothing Technology

IT Packages

Office: Microsoft Word, Excel, PowerPoint
Internet and email
Running of databases

Fiona Murie, FIMC CMC, MBA

Wheatland, Blackbush Rd, Round Hay Park, Leeds, LS17 9OD

Tel: 44 (0) 1132 xxx xxx, E-mail: fi@indepthcg.com or Fiona.murie@tiscali.co.uk

Twenty-seven years' experience in the Civil Service from operational and project management roles to strategy development and management consultancy. Lead by example using analysis and planning to get things done and gain further motivation from the positive response I receive.

Versatile leader

- Created a motivated team that accomplished all performance targets within £7m budget, reduced absence rates from 12% to 9.5% and achieved Charter Mark status. Effectively managed a busy operational unit with 300 staff processing 75,000 new claims for benefit and their ongoing maintenance. Challenged archaic processes, gave people freedom to execute new ideas, improved structure and encouraged collaboration. (2002/03)

- Fixed a failing project in Jobcentre Plus. Observed and questioned to understand roles and relationships with stakeholders. Reviewed team roles, restored partnerships and implemented a governance structure. Built a cohesive team focused on delivery of objectives and able to move the project forward. (2003/04)

Ability to analyze

- Brought together five businesses into one with 400 staff during a major change programme. Prioritized tasks and engaged with stakeholders. Developed organizational structure, identified high-level processes and implemented a strategy to align services. Successfully launched the new branch on schedule with a clearly understood plan of development. (2000)

- Created clarity for staff and forced senior managers to take responsibility and make decisions about the future of the project. Shaped a disorganized project where little progress had been made. Identified problems through discussion with stakeholders, produced project documentation, a comprehensive plan and implemented governance arrangements. (2004/05)

Deliver quality results

- Delivered the benefits realization strategy for a national IT project. Researched best practice then conducted in-depth interviews, organized and facilitated a workshop with all stakeholders, and produced the benefits realization plan. This helped secure continued resource and senior management commitment. My customer's evaluation said 'a star in the making who has delivered a first-rate job'. (2004)

- Transformed project plan and management of a major change project. Interviewed people to gain knowledge and examined best practice. Developed a working-level plan for all stakeholders and a strategic plan for the project board. Provided a solid and visible foundation for the project and focused discussion at board level. Subsequently adopted across all similar projects. (2002)

Inspire others

- Mentored two primary school head teachers as part of the 'Partners in Leadership Programme'. Gained an understanding of school life and the issues. Provided advice and guidance, shared knowledge and transferred skills. Head teacher's personal effectiveness was increased and gained valuable knowledge of a different management environment.

- Co-founder of a small informal network group of six women. Researched existing network groups and gauged level of support. Established remit, organized meetings, facilitated discussions and provided support and motivation. Without exception, everyone has developed professionally and personally. (2000 onwards)

Effective communicator

- Wrote report issued to the Prime Minister about Departmental progress. Analyzed assessments to understand the position and identify areas for improvement. Co-ordinated contributions from nine separate businesses, designed and facilitated a work-shop, drafted the progress report and improvement plan. Report agreed and signed-off by senior civil servants and delivered on time. (2005)

- Personally supported the Benefits Agency Chief Executive at two Public Accounts Committees. Examined Hansard and previous papers on similar hearings. Organized others to provide information, collated responses, compiled briefing and supported at the actual hearing. The Chief Executive was able to respond quickly and accurately, received his personal thanks and was rewarded for my contribution. (1998/99)

Career History

Twenty-seven years in the Department for Work and Pensions in the following roles:

Principal Managing Consultant	2004–present
Project Manager/Consultant	2003–2004
Operational Manager	2002–2003
Deputy Project Manager	2001–2002
Project Manager	2000–2001
Section Head	1999–2000
Strategic Manager	1995–1999
Various management roles	1987–1995
Various administrative roles	1979–1987

Professional Qualifications and Accreditation

Certificate in Consultancy Practice, Centre for Management & Policy Studies, 2005

Master of Business Administration, Leeds Metropolitan University, 2004

Certificate in Management, Leeds Metropolitan University, 2002

MBTI Practitioner, 2005

Certified Management Consultant, 2005

PRINCE2 Practitioner, 2003

Fellow of the Institute of Management Consultants, 2004

Michael Matthews

Hampstead Rd, London NW3

Tel: 44 (0) 207 xxx xxxx, E-mail: mjam@invest.co.uk

Strong-minded 21-year-old leader with a competitive streak and the aspiration to succeed at the highest level. Currently studying for the MSc Investments.

2004–2005   **The University of Birmingham, MSc Investments**

2001–2004   **BSc Econ (Hons) Banking and Finance, 2.1, University of Wales, Cardiff**

Teamwork and Leadership

- As Captain of Cardiff Business School RFC, steered the team to winning the Cardiff University Rugby League. Displayed dedication and assumed responsibility for on-field and off-field activities to generate an enjoyable and successful attitude amongst the squad. Key responsibilities included organizing and directing weekly training sessions, communicating with sport facility managers, and providing advice to squad members to improve performance and achieve productive results.

- Undergraduate banking project on 'the case for, and arguments against a free banking environment' produced in conjunction with three course members. Efficient time management allowed the group to meet on a weekly basis. At meetings tasks were delegated, for example specific academic areas to research, deadlines set and the findings discussed at each meeting. Allowed for the argument to be structured and powerful. Presented to academic staff and professionals with the result of the group significantly improving their degree result.

Energy and Motivation

- In 1999 successfully completed a 12-man expedition to Costa Rica. Eighteen months of fitness and fundraising preparation resulted in the ascent of Mount Chirripo and a community project assisting a research farm in its development. This project led to the construction of a much needed accommodation block and land cultivation.

- To develop leadership qualities completed an Army Leadership course during Easter 2000. Planning, briefing and commanding regular Army soldiers on a platoon mission greatly improved my communication and problem-solving skills. Additionally these skills were taken back to the cadet force where they were implemented to train recruits of the school's contingent.

Confidence and Decisiveness

- During the Presidency of Cardiff Business Society in 2003/4 member numbers were increased to 450 and sponsorship obtained from various businesses, including PricewaterhouseCoopers. This developed personal confidence to deal with others in a formal environment and also to present myself and my ideas concisely and confidently.

- As leader of several Army cadet teams in regional competitions, decisions on 'command tasks' enhanced the ability to make a confident decision quickly under pressure and to implement it through to completion. Approaching each situation individually and listening to the thoughts of others, plans were developed and executed resulting in a structured approach to the problems.

Handling Pressure

- Pressure to organize a successful Christmas Ball for Cardiff Business School and ensure ticket sales targets met in order to cover costs. Differentiating the evening from past events resulted in increased demand for tickets, targets met and an event enjoyed by all in attendance. Furthermore, the reputation of the Business School and the society was enhanced.

- In Sixth Form I was Sales Director of 'Fusion', a Young Enterprise company. The firm produced office products and sales targets had to be realistic and adhered to. Construction of a sales channel and direct marketing, which targeted teaching staff, parents and the public when we exhibited at the Merry Hill Shopping Centre near Stourbridge, ensured sales thrived. Liaising with the Finance Department guaranteed that the business operated within budget. Six months of trading and an examination resulted in enhanced knowledge of how business works and ultimately a profit generated for its shareholders.

Work Experience during Student Holidays

28/06/2004–09/07/2004 – Gateley Wareing, Birmingham
Two week internship spent across a variety of departments.

08/09/2004–12/09/2004 – Ashurt, Frankfurt
One week's work experience with a corporate partner.

Bill Faust

215 West, Brighton BN7 6PD, UK

M: 44 (0) xxx xxx H: 44 (0) 1273 xx xx xx E-mail: bill@pitchyourself.co.uk

I bring my zest for life to my work. I find solutions by understanding the questions that need to be asked. 18 years of practical integrated marketing ideas across many industry sectors from advertising to telecommunications throughout the world.

Concise Message Delivery

- Convey critical message to audiences at many of world's leading business schools based on the ideas from co-authored book *Pitch Yourself*. I engage the audience with my passion, belief and thorough understanding. Invited to talk at 50 of the Top 100 global business schools. (2005)

- Won new business of Fairfax, Australia's leading newspaper group when they approached Bates Advertising Agency. Devised and pitched a strategy that provided a seamless flow of information regardless of location or time zones, which allowed Fairfax to sell more media space more effectively than before.

Understanding the Questions to Ask

- Developed Working Links' (a Government PPP) new vision statement in alignment with all their stakeholders. Demonstrated how they could develop and expand into new markets by understanding why they had been so successful to date in their core employment market. (2003)

- Produced a strategy document for Orange's Mobile Portal, highlighting commercially viable revenue generation in a marketplace that nears full penetration of mobile devices. Understood the market issues, from the key drivers influencing the use of the mobile platform to revenue models. Studied all the content and services from customer and commercial points of view to the adoption of new technology. (2002)

Commercial Awareness

- Initiated and developed a business strategy to demonstrate the potential pet insurance portfolio of Pet Protect to £694 million pa, an increase of 488% to show it was a viable and saleable concern. (2000)

- Generated a strategic business concept for News Ltd that led to a successful commercial launch. Prepared competitive market analysis and produced the business plan covering all aspects from costs, head count, potential revenue growth to the fully specified functionality of the concept. (2000)

Provider of Innovative Solutions

- Co-authored the book *Pitch Yourself*: no. 67 on Top 100 Best Sellers and no. 4 Business Best Seller (amazon.co.uk) a new way to sell yourself to potential employers. Threw away the traditional CV rulebook and started from the ground up. Pitched concept to the publisher Prentice Hall (Pearson) delivering the book January 2002. Now in its second edition. *Pitch Yourself* is sold worldwide. (2001–2005)

- At Bates Advertising Agency in Australia (1999) I optimized a small budget through a pioneering 'Viral Marketing' campaign for Australia's leading chocolate biscuit Tim Tams. Achieved cult status and notoriety and endorsed by Tim Tams aficionados generating self-perpetuating PR.

Career History

Co-author of *Pitch Yourself* and Guest Speaker	2001 – date
Marketing Director: GEIH part of GE Capital	1999 to 2000 USA/UK
New Media Director: Bates Dorland	1998 to 1999 Australia
Head of Interactive: CIA media group	1997 to 1998 UK
Director, IMP (top 5 SP agency)	1996 to 1997 UK
Director, International Marketing: Yorkshire TV	1995 to 1996 UK
Account Director: U/C/M Ltd (new media agency)	1991 to 1995 UK
Rights Manager: Bayard Presse Paris	1990 to 1991 France
Advertisement Manager: Haymarket Publishing	1987 to 1990 UK

Education: Business Studies: Bournemouth University, UK.

Languages: Fluent Business French.

Ana Molina

10 Ocean Heights Drive, Brighton BN1 9OT

Tel: 44 (0) xxx xxx xxx

E-mail: anamolina@somewhere.com

I carefully consider each step I take. Twelve years of customer-focused roles from the retail environment to TV presenter and promotion work to fashion model.

Effective Communications and Attention to Detail

- Co-presented a live football programme and competition on terrestrial TV, Channel 37, interacting with both the studio audience and general public on the phone-in. To do this effectively I had to remain calm, polite and witty all within the constraints of live TV.

- Government project: 'The Introduction of the Euro in Spain'. My role was to make people feel comfortable with the Euro. At exhibitions and field marketing events showed public what the Euro looked like, how they could use it and its value compared to Pesetas. Overcame common issues from the belief their money was being devalued or that shops and restaurants would increase the prices of everyday essential goods and services. (2000)

Self-motivation and Motivating Others

- To apply for work as cabin crew with an international airline I knew I had to speak at least two languages fluently just to be considered. In November 2002 I came to England from Spain leaving my family and my career in promotions to learn English.

- Aerobics Instructor: The class was an effective exercise programme. It had to be fun and the best on offer. I achieved this through my enthusiasm, professional attitude and by gaining their trust: people wanted to come back again and again.

Team Player

- Red Cross Volunteer: Alicante Beach Patrol. There was a team of five; at all times there was one member in the watchtower, two in the patrol boat, one on beach patrol and one in the Red Cross tent. Each hour we rotated positions. We were the first people to get to the incidents and administered first aid for minor problems and stabilized more serious ones whilst waiting for the relevant emergency services.

- As a model I was part of a large organized team. To ensure the show's success everyone from the designers, hairdressers, makeup artists, to set designers and models had to be experts in their fields. We all worked under pressure and tight deadlines. We understood the importance of each person's input to ensure the show ran smoothly and on time. I could not have done my part without their expertise, help and co-operation as well as vice versa. (1994–2002)

Customer Relationships and Customer Care

- Involved in most aspects of my family's restaurant, *Casa Molina*, for the last six years from satisfying our customers' needs to waiting on tables, menu suggestions to kitchen work and taking care of staffing issues and requirements. (1998–present)

- Looked after guests, showing them all the behind the scenes action and all aspects of the race as a member of the client hospitality team for Astra Cycle Tour of Spain.

Organizational Agility

- Ensured the exhibition venue was correctly set up, stock was available, correct signage was in place, hotels booked for VIP guests and up-to-date tour information was available at each of the 20 destinations for the Astra Cycle Tour of Spain. (Sept 2003)

- Organized and confirmed the VIP guest list of top company directors for the Spanish Natural Gas Congress in Madrid. With the help of one other person worked to a tight timeline. We confirmed guest attendance via phone, e-mail and letter. 200 key guests attended, which ensured the event's success. (Sept–Nov 2001)

Career History

Waitress & Care Assistant at Brighton College   2004 to present

Studying English in Brighton   2002 to 2004

Promotions Work and Model   1994–2002

Astra, Volvo, Ericcson Mobile, Spanish Government (the Euro), Red Bull Photographic model

Casa Molina Restaurant (owned by my family) continuous involvement since 1998

Red Cross Volunteer: Beach Patrol   1996

TV Co-presenter   1995–97

Education

Bachillerato.

Languages

Spanish (mother tongue), English (fluent).

John Baldwin: Senior Mechanical Engineer

2 Doughton Rd, Gloucestershire, GL21 6PW

Mob: 44 (0) xxxx xxxx, Home: 44 (0) xxxx xxxx

E-mail: john@oilfield.com

Intelligent risk taker. Direction setter of inventive solutions with the willingness to absorb situations and get on with it. Thirty-one years leadership of $ multimillion mechanical engineering projects in the international oil industry.

Analytical communication

- My engineering background gives me an analytical nature. As GM and VP, I chaired weekly production meetings and successfully analyzed critical path processes to keep delivery schedules on track through the disruptive period of a plant expansion program.

- Participation in major tender authorship together with personal presentations to key account clients using communication skills dramatically improved bid package content and contributed to four new accounts and territory successes in a two-year period while maintaining all existing accounts.

Hands-on outside the box

- Eight years in Field Service Management in international offshore and onshore operations have given me a sound hands-on industry competency.

- GM Kvaerner Oilfield Products – Middle East. Instigated and set up a unique JV manufacturing partnership in Iran, resulting in a market entry over a four-year period, generating sales revenue of $5m. This continues to develop and grow. This was very much an 'outside the box' strategy not initially considered workable by some.

Supportive and approachable management style

- I managed 12 expatriate employees in three Middle Eastern countries, most of whom were family accompanied. I had responsibility for the equitable administration of company policy in areas such as housing, local benefits, schooling, vehicles, home leaves etc., requiring a fair and reasonable approach with even-handed treatment for all. Living conditions in the late 70s were trying and required a supportive and approachable management style.

- Joined Vetco in 2005 to increase their ability to manage and win strategic key accounts. Heightened visibility of Vetco to their customer base through my in-depth knowledge, experience of the oilfield equipment market and account management style. Giving customers the confidence and reassurance to invest their $multi-million dollar budgets with us.

Lateral move flexibility

- Accepted a lateral move as a career development opportunity and a chance to develop from scratch a complete Sales and Marketing presence where none had existed. This resulted in sales exceeding $5m/annum within two years and a threefold increase in headcount plus an additional district office setup.

- I am a well-rounded individual having demonstrated a flexibility that has progressed me through 10 senior positions, in 10 postings (six international) with three multinational companies that have required a solid mix of business and pleasure with colleagues and clients. Throughout, a supportive wife and family have ably encouraged me.

Career History

Vetco   2005 to present

Account Manager – based London

One of the world's largest manufacturers of oilfield equipment and tools

Kvaerner Oilfield Products   1996 to 2005

Regional Sales Manager Europe, Africa and Middle East, based Head Office London

General Manager Middle East – based Dubai

General Manager & Vice President Asia Pacific, based Singapore

FMC Corporation UK Ltd   1979 to 1995

Area Sales Manager Europe & North Africa, Key Account Manager, based London

Regional Sales Manager, Europe, Africa and Middle East, based France

Key Account Manager, based London

Regional Sales Manager Australasia, based Melbourne

McEvoy Oilfield Equipment Ltd   1973 to 1979

Senior Sales Engineer, based Singapore

Sales and Service Manager, based Scotland

Peglar Hattersley and Newman Hender Ltd   1966 to 1973

Languages

English, fluent Business French

Albertus (Bert) Zwiers

Gastelseweg 10-f

2389 RS The Hague, The Netherlands

Mobile: + 31 (0) xxx xxx, Home: + 31 (0) xxx xx xx

E-mail: bertzwiers@home.nl

Authentic and inspiring business leader, delivers prominent results by bringing out the best in his people. Managing Director of five years with comprehensive international experience.

Outperformer (delivers outstanding performance, superior quality and innovation)

- Targeted to grow Flender Bruinhof's gross margin by 30% in 2 years; analyzed market, identified opportunity for international expansion; doubled revenue from international service activities; increased gross margin by 40%. (July 2004)

- Planned 20% lower overhead in 2 business years; designed and implemented a lean organizational structure and enhanced business processes; a 40% higher gross margin and a 20% lower overhead doubled operational profits. (July 2004)

Strategic and analytical thinker (able to spot trends and patterns and synthesize direction)

- Identified opportunity to access a high-end complementary market; built a strategic alliance with Schelde Gears to gain access to the naval defence industry; diversified Flender's product portfolio and jump-started Flender's R&D activities. (August 2004)

- Tasked to reduce cost of sales by 10% at Flender Bruinhof; identified opportunity to merge 3 national sales companies; developed full-scale merger proposal with planned net savings in excess of 1 million Euro per annum. (May 2003)

Team Leader (proven ability to manage well across culturally diverse teams)

- Assigned by Smit to realize long-term marine charters for Sakhalin Energy; developed international project organization on Sakhalin and in Singapore; selected, trained and assigned multinational teams; met Client's specifications in full. (April 1999)

- Tasked at Shell to build an effective US East Coast marine spill response organization; built, trained and exercised readiness of a regional response team; responded effectively to 2 actual spills as on-site team leader; handled press communications. (May 1994)

Ambassador and Networker (proven ability to cement fruitful relationships)

- Natural authority allowed for an explicitly good business environment at Flender.

- Natural skill when communicating with staff, clients and other stakeholders.

- Assigned to develop a new market for Lloyd's Register; researched targeted companies and identified their needs, developed niche product; networked with decision makers; captured 90% of the market as targeted using first-mover advantage. (August 1997)

Innovator and Change Agent

- Identified synergy-based opportunity in Shell's and Mobil's oil product distribution networks in the US Northeast; initiated an innovative joint venture; reduced Shell's direct distribution costs with more than US$5 million per annum. (April 1995)

- Planned to improve Flender's gear delivery performance by 50% in 2 years; researched business processes; designed and delivered an innovative restructuring project; gear delivery performance improved to over 90%. (July 2004)

Career

1999 – 2004	Managing Director at A. Friedr. Flender AG (Bruinhof B.V.) in Rotterdam
1997 – 1999	Fleet Director at Smit International in Singapore
1995 – 1997	Manager Business Development at Lloyd's Register in Rotterdam
1993 – 1995	Marine Superintendent at Shell Oil Company in Houston
1991 – 1993	Manager Regional Response at Shell Oil Company in Houston
1989 – 1991	Ship Assessor at Shell International Marine in London
1974 – 1989	Maritime Officer at Shell Tankers in Rotterdam

Qualifications

2005	Executive Master of Business Administration, Rotterdam School of Management
1996	Lead Auditor ISO 9000/14000, Institute of Quality Assurance
1991	Chartered Shipbroker, Institute of Chartered Shipbrokers
1986	Certificate of Competency as Master Mariner (Class 1 Foreign Going)
1979	Certificate of Competency as Marine Engineer (Class 3 Steam & Motor)

Service to the Community

Chairman of the Professor Gielen Foundation, managing seven primary schools

Treasurer of the Royal Standard of Peter the Great Maritime Education Trust

Member of the Advisory Board of the AHOY Rotterdam Maritime exhibition

Personal Details

Date of birth 18 June 1955, Dutch nationality, married, one daughter

KEN LIVINGSTONE: MAYOR OF LONDON

Running the City of London is my dream job. I am 100% committed to improving the life of each and every Londoner. I lead from the front, getting to the root of each issue. I am prepared to stand up to big government for the people of London. 16 years as both a Member of the UK Parliament for the Labour Party and the Mayor for London.

Gaining Loyalty and Building Working Relationships

I give my commitment. I never withdraw it even if I might like to change my mind. I strive to gain a consensus of opinion and act accordingly. The £7 billion Cross Rail 'Heathrow to Docklands' project demonstrates my total commitment to building successful working relationships across the private and public sectors (central government, city and local councils).

Long-Range Thinking

Transport policies for the capital are not overnight fixes. To successfully solve the capital's transport issues I need to exercise interlocking policies that vary in size, manner and approach from 5 to 15 years for the major schemes.

Employing Giants

I am not afraid to employ giants. The only important issue is to get the very best person to take on the challenge and fulfil the role to its full potential. The London Underground is a classic example. One of my proudest achievements was getting Bob Kiley, a giant in urban transport who reformed the New York subway, to join my team.

Quick Decision Making

I was elected to make a difference. I made a promise to ease the congestion in the capital and congestion charges for traffic entering the capital are the answer. I believe in it and believe it is best for London. Government ministers urged me to delay this decision until after the next mayoral election. I went ahead and kept my promise because I believe Londoners had a right to see if it worked before they voted again in the mayoral election.

Tactician

Napoleon said he sacked generals 'if they were not lucky'. You need luck and you need tactics. When I first stood in the London mayoral election as an independent, 10 weeks out, four of my five key advisors said I would lose as the press would destroy me. However, the press concentrated on my Labour opposition Frank Dobson for the first 9 of the 10 weeks. Only in the last week did the press turn their attention on me. Luck or tactics? The right tactics generate luck.

Re-elected Mayor of London in June 2004.

Dealing with Conflict

Find out the real issue or grievance and solve it. Do not drag it out. Find the common ground. State what is impossible. You are left with what is possible and you get straight to the point.

Career History

Elected Mayor of London	2000 to present
Labour MP for Brent East	1987 to 2000
Elected Leader of the GLC	1981 to 1986
Elected Labour member of the GLC	1973 to 1981
Member of Camden Council	1978 to 1982
Labour Member of Lambeth Council	1971 to 1978
Technician, Chester Beatty Cancer Research Institute	1963 to 1971

Author of:

If Voting Changed Anything They'd Abolish It (Collins, 1987)
Livingstone's Labour (Unwin Hyman, 1989)

MARC SCHAVEMAKER:
Commercial Airline Pilot (Boeing 737/747)

Jupiter Laan 64, 1644XS Haarlem, NL

Tel: 23 (0) 429 xxxx, E-mail: marc@skyport.nl

I continually increase my ability to deal with the fast-moving complex situations, whilst inspiring confidence in others around me. I have developed a solid foundation in safety procedures and people management. I worked in industry for 6 years as a chartered civil engineer prior to becoming an airline pilot 7 years ago.

The competencies I use on a daily basis whilst flying for the 'World's Favourite Airline' British Airways are:

Ability to Lead

An airline pilot must show leadership and commercial awareness in the management of the day-to-day operation, providing a safe efficient service. The ability to make decisions is based on available information, experience and intuition. I take a leading role and seek to discuss steps I would take in resolving situations. This results in the building of experience and confidence, providing a greater number of appropriate suggestions on operational issues.

Situational Awareness and Lateral Thinking

It is essential to build a mental model of your surroundings. Continual monitoring of the aircraft systems, maintaining spatial awareness and constant liaison with all the crew increases my capacity to deal with any event that may occur.

Organizational Ability and Agility

It is essential to organize my tasks effectively to reduce my workload and increase my capacity. I have the presence of mind and forethought to prioritize and carry out multiple tasks simultaneously whilst maintaining accuracy. Achieved by planning actions, working logically and thinking ahead. I am then of greater assistance to my crew and can maintain smooth operation of the service.

Effective Communications

The need to convey and receive information succinctly is a must. Effective briefing techniques are imperative for a successful flight from the ground up (and down again). I have an approachable style and carry out my tasks in accordance with the Standard Operating Procedures whilst liaising with all my fellow crew in an open and co-operative manner, resulting in a reduction of inherent risk and shared knowledge.

Technical and Practical Aptitude

I must be fundamentally familiar with the aircraft. I have an awareness and willingness to keep up to date with the aircraft systems and handling characteristics. When situations allow, I make the most of handling the aircraft. I study regularly to keep abreast of all relevant material ensuring I am up to date with all aspects of the aircraft's technical data. This increases my confidence of the aircraft's capabilities allowing me to be better prepared for all scenarios.

Ability to Promote Good Teamwork

To maintain a good overall situational awareness and create an effective harmonious team, it is important to create an open and efficient working environment utilizing 'Crew Resource Management'. This maximizes the effectiveness of the whole crew. I must recognize the skills of others and complement them to my own through consultation and delegation furthering our skill base. The result is to reduce the workload of all crew members providing an increased capacity to focus on safety and efficiency.

Career History

British Airways   1998 to present
  Flying 747   2003 to present
  Flying 737   1998 to 2003

NRA & Environment Agency   1991 to 1998

Education

Civil Engineering Degree

LOUISE MEDLEY: Sales Professional

The Stables Lock, Yaynings, UK.

Tel: 44 (0) 1592 xxx xxx, Email: lou@freestyle.com

A clear thinking and a common sense approach has been vital in my 14-year sales career and allowed me to deliver over £1.5 million of sales last year.

- 'Self starter and works well on her own initiative.' Manager's Annual Review (IBP)

- 'Louise is dependable and a key member of the team and very hardworking.' Manager's Yearly Review of Performance (BSS)

Sales Negotiation

- Reached and exceeded sales target of £1.5 million in 2005. Convinced contractors, engineers, and distributors of the benefits of IBP as a supplier of low-price, high-volume products with limited room for price negotiations.

- At BSS (UK) Ltd increased sales volume by 20% without decreasing the profit margins on each sale. Strengthened customer relations after market research identified negotiation opportunities in non-price sensitive areas from payment terms to speed of delivery.

Relationship/Partnership Building

- Comprehensively understood and met the needs of specifiers, users and distributors across a complex sales chain, resulting in £1.5 million sales at IBP.

- Produced solid customer base that returned, time after time, and generated a personal sales turnover of £2 million. Developed long-term relationships based on trust and quality of service. Key importance was to keep up to date with local events and future proposed projects. Continual assessment and servicing of the companies and their contractors was a must. (BSS 1998 to 2001)

Customer Care

- Introduced range of new products across specifier, user and distributor sales chain. Kept abreast of breaking industry knowledge in order to provide our customers with the products they need.

- Developed bespoke sales solutions that enabled me to exceed sales target by 20% at BSS (UK) Ltd. Tailored specific sales plans to fulfil customer requests from delivery to aftercare service through listening, understanding their needs and by being available. Increased their confidence in BSS to supply exact requirements resulting in further sales.

Ability to Spot Patterns and Trends

- Produced efficient sales environments enabling me to exceed sales targets at both IBP and BSS (1991 to 2005). Detailed scrutiny to discover the market movements and predict the next growth area was carried out for all sales information, external market factors and reports. Acted instantly on the analysis, giving customer base the right product on time and at the right price.

- Built Freestyle Frenzie, a thriving dance community, from scratch and sold it as a going concern in the first quarter of 2001. Identified opportunity in 1998 and over 3 years achieved target levels of foot fall, met expectations of guests, created venue and promotional plans and monitored P&L.

Career History

Vent-Axia: **Residential Sales Executive from 2006**

Manufacturers of ventilation systems with 65% of the UK market.

IBP Conex: **Specification Manager 2001 to 2005**

Market leading manufacturer of copper fittings, for domestic, commercial and industrial use.

Role: Increase IBP sales in the South Coast area through specification and contractor selling and to improve coverage of stocks through the domestic and commercial merchant networks.

Duties included:

Market Research of both customer and competitor information

Client Relationship Management

Regular customer servicing to ensure excellent network

Monitoring and updating project tracking system

Production of sales and promotional literature

Promoting IBP at PHEX, DHPTE and Channel Island exhibitions

Presentation and training on IBP products at universities

Demonstrations to trade press, contractors, consultants and local authorities

BSS (UK) Ltd: **Sales Representative 1991 to 2001**

Leading distributor and largest UK pipeline and process equipment company – annual turnover £416 million. Held four key support and sales positions and was promoted three times.

Role: Promote BSS, its products and services to existing and new customers continually review markets and products in conjunction with Regional Sales Manager.

Duties included:

Solution selling

Product sales

Negotiation of terms

Market research of both customer and competitor information

Client Relationship Management

Monitoring and updating project tracking system

Administration

Remotely manage third party suppliers

Freestyle Frenzie: **Set up and sold 1998 to 2001**

Dance Company specialized in modern jive and dirty dancing

Education

Open University – Degree in Humanities   **Feb 2003 – present**

Currently studying. Completed 2 years of a 6-year course.

BTEC National Certificate in Business & Finance   **Sept 1994 – June 1996**

Qualification obtained by attending Brighton College of Technology in the evenings.

Personal

Married with one daughter. Enjoy playing tennis, dancing and swimming.

LAURA NEILSON

Helicopter House, Merryfield, Nr Taunton, Somerset

Tel: 01884 xxx xxx, E-mail: laura@elsewhere.co.uk

I have a calm and considered approach to my life. A qualified Veterinary Nurse of 11 years. If I could, I would ride my horse to work.

Commercial Awareness

- To grow and maintain the position of market leader of Hills Prescription Diets by providing individual sales plans and practice protocols to each practice. After every operation performed on a dog the owner is supplied with a 'recovery pack', building awareness and increasing sales of the Gastro Intestinal Diet.

- Increased the number of pet insurance policies sold via participating veterinary practices. Made decisions on which practices were most likely to produce extra policy sales and provided these with promotional material, training and support. Generated both new policies and further practices that wanted to participate in the scheme. (Pet Protect 2000)

Building and Influencing Relationships

- Regularly visit, inform, train the practices on 'prescription and life stage diets' and provide promotional offers in order for Hills Pet Nutrition to stay no. 1 and be 'The Vet's no. 1 choice to feed their own pets'. (2005)

- Pet Protect became the pet insurance company of choice in 444 practices, out of 700 in my region. Had to ascertain which practices were forward thinking and insurance minded. Built strong relationships with practices, provided a service second to none and supplied in-house staff training, demonstrating the benefits of the policies for both pet owners and practices. Practice staff became confident in the insurance policy to recommend building a further bond of trust with their customers. Win–win scenario for all. (1998 to 2001)

Effective Communications and Negotiations

- Professional Teaching Qualification: Certificate in City and Guilds Coaching & Assessing Individuals. This is awarded to those teaching and working with candidates for their vocational NVQ (National Vocational Qualification).

- Increased number of new practice trials and increased the number of insurance policies produced from existing practices on average by 10%. Gained required shelf space to promote the insurance products in practices throughout region. Matched the practice needs to the features and benefits and back-up systems of the product, ensuring efficient service. Put in place an award/incentive scheme for practice staff and the practice as a whole and ensured efficient running of back office processes at Pet Protect, for example, on receipt of a claim payments being made to the practice within 48 hrs etc.

Organizational Agility

Freed up an additional 20 hours of time per month, ensuring vets could be vets and nurses could be nurses. Benchmarked similar practices around the UK, studied last two years of practice records and discovered certain trends. Devised new staff rotas to take advantage of the patterns and freed staff up to concentrate on their core responsibilities and not be diverted to unproductive tasks. Greater efficiency and savings made as nursing team were available for theatre, consulting, hospitalised patients, practice administration etc. Led to the smooth running of a team of seven nurses in a busy mixed country practice. (The Veterinary Group 1998)

Career History

Hills Pet Nutrition – Veterinary Territory Manager 2001 to present

Market leader in supplying vets with prescription diets for their customers. Owned by Colgate Palmolive Group.

Pet Protect – Regional Veterinary Manager, 1998 to 2001

Subsidiary of GE Financial Insurance and ranked no. 2 in the pet insurance market. To increase distribution network amongst the veterinary practices.

The Veterinary Group – Head Veterinary Nurse, 1989 to 1998

Professional Qualifications

Veterinary Nursing Diploma

Certificate in City & Guilds Coaching & Assessing Individuals

CHRISTINE COLEMAN
76 Street, Upper West, NY

Phone (UK): 44 (0) XXXXXXX. Phone (US): 1 212-XXX-XXXX
Email: cc@luxuryretail.com

I tackle the real issues by having an open mind and understanding what and who is around me. Seven years of international experience in the luxury goods industry and a solid formal education culminating in the completion of my MBA in 2005.

Ability to Deliver Results

- Exceeded Crème de la Mar sales target by 25% and built a strong relationship with key Saks $multimillion account. Built a loyal-end user client base that fitted the ideal customer profiles of both CdlM & Saks. Managed internal and external teams, organized events to encourage usage of product and in store footfall. Preferred supplier status achieved and was invited to take part in Saks' PR events along with other preferred luxury goods suppliers.

- Exceeded 2002 annual sales target for Revive, exclusively distributed by Neiman Marcus in Florida, by 15%. Broadened product knowledge of Revive, through training of both exclusive sales consultants and staff in related departments including women's fashion, designers and the cosmetics departments, to cross sell Revive and became the preferred product of choice. Spotted opportunity to increase footfall to concession through proposing and agreeing new location within three months with both senior management of both Revive and NM.

- Created and implemented new strategy that increased sales of Revive Lip & Perioral Renewal Cream by 50%. Maximised the niche market of 18–25 years by teaming up with two market leading cosmetic brands. Opened up the opportunity to introduce Revive products to a larger number of this new and lucrative market.

Leadership through trust

- Created an environment were individuals felt their input was of true value in building the business through constantly meeting the needs of each individual and continuously involving the team in the decision making process. (Revive 2002)

- Increased efficiency of the team and enabled them to exceed their targets by 25%. Motivated my team and encouraged them to freely express their opinions as instigated an open-door policy where they understood I would be receptive to any new ideas in a personable and empathetic manner. (CdIM 2001)

Passionate Communication

- Structured and presented Art History monthly seminar program; selected art works and presented to peers and professional academics. Ensured all aspects of the seminar were understood through incisive passion and encouraged interaction and questions. (MA in Art History)

- Wrote and presented a weekly three hour classical radio show on WPRK, a mainstream local radio station with an audience of over 80,000 listeners. Held and organized weekly listener call and in contest (p/t 2000)

Staff Development and Training

- Ensured corporate sales message was consistent across the distribution network. Devised, wrote and presented training seminars to new recruits and existing staff on the corporate structure and complete product range. After each presentation held detailed Q & A sessions. Sales team were shown how to combine Revive products with other luxury goods in store that increased average unit sale. This helped maintain preferred supplier status of Revive at Neiman Marcus. (2002)

- Increased the annual sales 10% with the introduction of an employee incentive-based scheme at Clinique. Ensured team had the best product knowledge enabling them to promote the range directly and via inter-selling. Held seminars to keep them updated on latest trends, company information and events. Each month the individuals with the highest sales were rewarded.

WORK HISTORY

2002–2003 **Account Manager, Revive Skincare, Neiman Marcus, Orlando, FL**

- In charge of marketing, promotions, budgets and targets.
- Provided monthly qualitative and quantitative business reports
- Trained staff on merchandise and created incentives for sales assistants
- Responsible for customer relationship management

2000–2002 **Business Managers, Crème De La Mar, Saks Fifth Avenue, Orlando, FL**

- Developed external and internal client base
- Trained and supervised sales assistant
- Participated in product presentation and detailing
- Accountable for achieving monthly and annual sales targets

1998–2000 **Product Specialist, Clinique, Saks Fifth Avenue, Orlando, FL**

- Responsible for employee education and training on brand
- Organized and executed educational workshops for staff
- Developed and maintained client database

1996–1998 **Make-up Artist, Chanel Cosmetics, Dillards, Orlando, FL**

1993–1995 **Lisa Maile Modelling and Judy Venn Talent Agency Modelling Designers**

- Calvin Klein, Guess, Ralph Lauren, DKNY, Nicole Miller, Escada, Tadashi, BCBG Max Azria, Lily Pulitzer, Dana Buchman, Liz Claiborne, Tommy Hilfiger, Lacoste, Diana von Furstenberg

EDUCATION

2004–2005	Masters in Business Administration, University of Glasgow, Scotland
2003–2004	Masters of Arts in History of Art, University of York, England
1999–2003	Bachelor of Arts in Humanities, Rollins College, Winter Park, Florida
2003	(Internship) Assistant to Education Coordinator: Cornell Fine Arts Museums Helped develop art education programs for children and adults
2003	Docent: Albin Polsek Museum, Winter Park, Florida

chapter

The beginning

Pitch Yourself drags the recruitment process into the twenty-first century, dismantling 100 years of tradition. It provides, for the first time ever, an integrated approach to getting the job you really want. It transforms the way you sell yourself.

Your Elevator Pitch proves you are the best person to hire by clearly defining and articulating your benefit to their organization in a consistent and cumulative manner at each step of the recruitment process.

You directly answer 'What do you offer me?' by identifying, evaluating and innovatively bundling your Transferable Assets to prove:

➡ You are their 'how'

➡ You are their 'who'

➡ You have the 'what'

➡ You have been at the 'where'

You've matched what you're selling to your next employer with what they are buying by knowing and understanding your Transferable Assets and by knowing how and when to present the strongest and most relevant aspects to them. You've established a common language that aligns your focus from the past to the future and from your perspective to their perspective in a structured manner at each step of the recruitment process.

You've created the building blocks for your Elevator Pitch that can be used to customize and quickly build a new Elevator Pitch for each new opportunity you have. You want to write a cover letter, prepare for an interview, fill in an application form or write your new Elevator Pitch CV? You can.

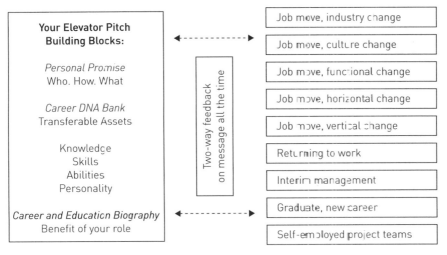

Figure 6.1 The universality of your Elevator Pitch

Your Elevator Pitch is designed to be flexible to meet your needs in today's dynamic working environments. It bundles and communicates your Transferable Assets – the source of your present and future value – in a relevant and targeted way. It enables you to successfully position yourself at each step of your job hunt, shortening and sharpening the entire process.

Your Elevator Pitch helps you cross industries, functions, cultures and geographies as shown in Figure 6.1. It helps you move horizontally or vertically and to return to work or take a career break. It unites variety and highlights singularity.

Everything you need to know, say and do.

The most effective CV you'll ever write. It gets read. You get noticed.

The best interview you'll ever give. You get noticed.

Secure the job you really want.

brilliant CV
second edition
Jim Bright
0273702114
April 2005

Based on actual research into what employers and recruiters want to see, *Brilliant CV* is an international bestseller and the UK's bestselling CV book. Now the fully updated and revised second edition reveals three new chapters and all the latest research. The number one CV guide has just got better!

brilliant interview
second edition
Ros Jay
0273703560
May 2005

What do interviewers really want from a candidate? How do they decide whether to hire you or someone else? Who better to advise interviewees than interviewers? Arm yourself with the advantage of knowing what interviewers are looking for and how to supply it.

Like *Brilliant CV*, this book is highly practical and interactive, with features such as tips from the experts, shining examples, horror stories, questions and quizzes to get you thinking. Learn to show yourself in the best possible light and maximise your chances of getting the job.

Guaranteed to propel you into your dream job!

If you wish to find out more about any of these titles or view our full list visit us at:
www.pearson-books.com